Cognitive–Behavioral Therapy

Theories of Psychotherapy Series

Theories of Psychotherapy Series

Jon Carlson and Matt Englar-Carlson, Series Editors

Cognitive–Behavioral Therapy

Michelle G. Craske

American Psychological Association

Washington, DC

Second Printing, December 2010

Published by
American Psychological Association
750 First Street, NE
Washington, DC 20002
www.apa.org

To order
APA Order Department
P.O. Box 92984
Washington, DC 20090-2984
Tel: (800) 374-2721; Direct: (202) 336-5510
Fax: (202) 336-5502; TDD/TTY: (202) 336-6123
Online: www.apa.org/books/
E-mail: order@apa.org

In the U.K., Europe, Africa, and the Middle East, copies may be ordered from
American Psychological Association
3 Henrietta Street
Covent Garden, London
WC2E 8LU England

Typeset in Minion by Shepherd Inc., Dubuque, IA

Printer: Edwards Brothers, Ann Arbor, MI
Cover Designer: Minker Design, Sarasota, FL
Cover Art: *Lily Rising*, 2005, oil and mixed media on panel in craquelure frame, by Betsy Bauer.

The opinions and statements published are the responsibility of the authors, and such opinions and statements do not necessarily represent the policies of the American Psychological Association.

Library of Congress Cataloging-in-Publication Data

Craske, Michelle G.
 Cognitive-behavioral therapy / Michelle G. Craske.
     p. cm.
 Includes bibliographical references and index.
 ISBN-13: 978-1-4338-0548-6
 ISBN-10: 1-4338-0548-0
 1. Cognitive therapy. 2. Behavior therapy. I. Title.
 RC489.C63C73 2010
 616.89'1425--dc22
                    2009018747

British Library Cataloguing-in-Publication Data
A CIP record is available from the British Library.

Printed in the United States of America
First Edition

Contents

Series Preface

Some might argue that in the contemporary clinical practice of psychotherapy, evidence-based intervention and effective outcome have overshadowed theory in importance. Maybe. But, as editors of this series, we don't propose to take up that controversy here. We do know that psychotherapists adopt and practice according to one theory or another because their experience, and decades of good evidence, suggests that having a sound theory of psychotherapy leads to greater therapeutic success. Still, the role of theory in the helping process can be hard to explain. This narrative about solving problems helps convey theory's importance:

> Aesop tells the fable of the sun and wind having a contest to decide who was the most powerful. From above the earth, they spotted a man walking down the street, and the wind said that he bet he could get his coat off. The sun agreed to the contest. The wind blew and the man held on tightly to his coat. The more the wind blew, the tighter he held. The sun said it was his turn. He put all of his energy into creating warm sunshine and soon the man took off his coat.

What does a competition between the sun and the wind to remove a man's coat have to do with theories of psychotherapy? We think this deceptively simple story highlights the importance of theory as the precursor to any effective intervention—and hence to a favorable outcome. Without a guiding theory, we might treat the symptom without understanding the role of the individual. Or we might create power conflicts with our clients and not understand that, at times, indirect means of helping (sunshine) are often as effective—if not more so—than direct ones (wind). In the absence of theory, we might lose track of the treatment focus and instead get caught up in, for example, social correctness and not wanting to do something that looks too simple.

What exactly *is* theory? The *APA Dictionary of Psychology* defines theory as "a principle or body of interrelated principles that purports to explain or predict a number of interrelated phenomena." In psychotherapy, a theory is a set of principles used to explain human thought and behavior, including what causes people to change. In practice, a theory creates the goals of therapy and specifies how to pursue them. Haley (1997) noted that a theory of psychotherapy ought to be simple enough for the average therapist to understand but comprehensive enough to account for a wide range of eventualities. Furthermore, a theory guides action toward successful outcomes while generating hope in both the therapist and client that recovery is possible.

Theory is the compass that allows psychotherapists to navigate the vast territory of clinical practice. In the same ways that navigational tools have been modified to adapt to advances in thinking and ever-expanding territories to explore, theories of psychotherapy have changed over time. The different schools of theories are commonly referred to as *waves*, the first wave being psychodynamic theories (i.e., Adlerian, psychoanalytic), the second wave learning theories (i.e., behavioral, cognitive–behavioral), the third wave humanistic theories (person-centered, gestalt, existential), the fourth wave feminist and multicultural theories, and the fifth wave postmodern and constructivist theories. In many ways, these waves represent how psychotherapy has adapted and responded to changes in psychology, society, and epistemology as well as to changes in the nature of psychotherapy itself. Psychotherapy and the theories that guide it are dynamic and responsive. The wide variety of theories is also testament to the different ways in which the same human behavior can be conceptualized (Frew & Spiegler, 2008).

It is with these two concepts in mind—the central importance of theory and the natural evolution of theoretical thinking—that we developed the APA Theories of Psychotherapy Series. Both of us are thoroughly fascinated by theory and the range of complex ideas that drive each model. As university faculty members who teach courses on the theories of psychotherapy, we wanted to create learning materials that not only highlight the essence of the major theories for professionals and professionals in training but that also clearly bring the reader up to date on the current status of the models. Often in books on theory, the biography of the original theorist overshadows the evolution of the model. In contrast, our intent was to highlight the contemporary uses of the theories as well as their history and context.

As this project began, we faced two immediate decisions: which theories to address and who best to present them. We looked at graduate-level theories of psychotherapy courses to see which theories are being taught, and we explored popular scholarly books, articles, and conferences to determine which theories draw the most interest. We then developed a dream list of authors from among the best minds in contemporary theoretical practice. Each author is one of the leading proponents of that approach as well as a knowledgeable practitioner. We asked each author to review the core constructs of the theory, bring the theory into the modern sphere of clinical practice by looking at it through a context of evidence-based practice, and clearly illustrate how the theory looks in action.

There are 24 titles planned for the series. Each title can stand alone or can be put together with a few other titles to create materials for a course in psychotherapy theories. This option allows instructors to create a course featuring the approaches they believe are the most salient today. To support this end, APA Books has also developed a DVD for each of the approaches that demonstrates the theory in practice with a real client. Some of the DVDs show therapy over six sessions. Contact APA Books for a complete list of available DVD programs (http://www.apa.org/videos).

In *Cognitive–Behavioral Therapy*, Dr. Michelle Craske shows why CBT has become the most popular model of psychotherapy used in contemporary clinical practice. She highlights clinical research to support the efficacy of CBT with numerous populations and conditions. In addition to the focus on evidence-based practice, Dr. Craske provides case examples to depict how the CBT model works from a process perspective. Because of the widespread adoption of this model by clinicians and training programs alike, *Cognitive–Behavioral Therapy* is an important addition to the Theories of Psychotherapy Series.

REFERENCES

Frew, J., & Spiegler, M. (2008). *Contemporary psychotherapies for a diverse world*. Boston: Lahaska Press.

Haley, J. (1997). *Leaving home: The therapy of disturbed young people*. New York: Routledge.

Cognitive–Behavioral Therapy

1

Introduction

The hallmark features of cognitive–behavioral therapy (CBT) are short term, problem-focused cognitive and behavioral intervention strategies that are derived from the science and theory of learning and cognition. Also, the CBT approach to treatment implementation and evaluation is guided by principles of empirical science. The behavioral interventions aim to decrease maladaptive behaviors and increase adaptive ones by modifying their antecedents and consequences and by behavioral practices that result in new learning. Examples of behavioral interventions include behavioral activation for depression, problem solving for stress management, behavioral rehearsal for social skills deficits, and relaxation training and systematic exposure to anxiety-producing situations for anxiety disorders. The cognitive interventions aim to modify maladaptive cognitions, self-statements, or beliefs. The cognitive methods include identification of situational misappraisals and underlying distorted beliefs; rational disputation or logical consideration of the evidence to refute such misappraisals and core beliefs; behavioral practices designed to collect further data to disconfirm such misappraisals; and the generation of alternative, more evidence-based appraisals and core beliefs. Together, these cognitive and behavioral interventions have been shown to be effective for a number of different psychological disorders and conditions, including anxiety disorders, depression, personality disorders, substance use related disorders, eating disorders, pain management, couples distress, and aspects of psychosis. Indeed, CBT is considered to have the most evidence base of all psychosocial therapies (Roth & Fonagy, 1996).

The origins of CBT are in the science and theory of classical and instrumental conditioning, or learning theory. Within these theories, emphasis was given to the role of the reinforcing and punishing consequences that guide voluntary behaviors (e.g., positively reinforcing effects of euphoria upon continued drug consumption) as well as responses that become conditional due to associations with innately evocative events (e.g., development of fears of driving following a car accident). Originally, little consideration was given to the role of appraisals or thoughts as determinants of behaviors or emotions, although thoughts could be viewed as "another behavior" and therefore subject to the same rules of reinforcement and conditional responding.

Dissatisfaction with a strictly behavioral set of principles coincided with a rise in interest in cognitive principles that was spurred by social learning theory. This led to the content of judgments and underlying belief systems about the self and the world being given credence as determinants of emotion and action. Furthermore, the cognitive movement was fostered by advances in instrumental and classical conditioning theories that led to recognition of cognition as a potential mediator of learning. Thus, behavioral therapy became cognitive–behavioral therapy, all the while maintaining a science-based approach to the implementation of treatment, but now extending from behaviors to judgments and beliefs as targets of intervention. The science of cognition and information processing developed separately from the rise of cognitive therapy, and as described throughout this book, the former has raised significant questions regarding the purported mechanisms of the latter. Partly as a consequence of this questioning, recent "third wave" developments are reemphasizing behavioral principles and de-emphasizing the *content* of cognition.

In practice, individual clinicians vary in the degree to which they embrace behavioral as compared to cognitive principles and interventions. Some clinicians remain more behaviorally focused, and treat cognitions within a behavioral framework, such as by giving more emphasis to the function rather than the content of judgments and stated beliefs. The latter is particularly characteristic of the third wave therapies, such as acceptance and commitment therapy, which may be more appropriately termed *behavior therapy* rather than CBT. Other clinicians take an integrative approach, combining behavioral principles and interventions with cognitive principles and methods designed to modify the content of cognition. Still others are more cognitively focused and view the content of cognition as the driving factor behind all behaviors and emotions and as the primary focus of all therapeutic effort. The latter approach generally is referred to as *cognitive therapy*. However, cognitive therapists rely on behavioral methodologies to obtain evidence for disconfirmation or disputation of maladaptive cognitions. Hence, it is hard, if not impossible, to distinguish between cognitive therapy and CBT. Behavioral therapies that de-emphasize the content of cognition can be more readily distinguished from CBT, yet even here the distinction is sometimes hard to draw. For example, within behavioral interventions based on instrumental learning theory, thoughts can be regarded as antecedents to behaviors. Hence, if a set of verbal statements is an antecedent that elicits maladaptive behavior, then treatment aims to replace those statements with "alternative antecedent statements" that elicit more adaptive behavior. Clearly, such behavioral strategies overlap with cognitive strategies.

Thus, whereas more behaviorally versus more cognitively oriented clinicians rely on somewhat different principles for treatment formulation and understanding therapeutic change, they may use the same procedures for intervention. Conversely, both behavioral theory and cognitive theory principles can be evoked to explain therapeutic change with the same intervention strategy. As an example, behavioral theory attributes the effects of repeated exposure to feared situations to extinction of conditional fear responses; in accordance with cognitive theory, the same method of exposure serves to gather information that disconfirms mistaken judgments about danger.

Despite these variations in emphasis on behavioral and cognitive principles and methodologies, the CBT approach is unified by its empirical foundation, its reliance on the theory and science of behavior and cognition, and its problem-focused orientation. Whatever the emphasis given to behavioral or cognitive principles, the CBT therapist aims to replace maladaptive behaviors, emotions, and cognitions with more adaptive ones. Also, the CBT therapist accomplishes that aim within the context of ongoing evaluation of the effectiveness of intervention strategies and their modification, when necessary, to achieve optimal effects.

CBT is used widely by clinicians. For example, of 591 APA members who were randomly surveyed, 45.4% regarded themselves as CBT in theoretical orientation (Stewart & Chambless, 2007). This rate exceeded the rates for all other theoretical orientations, including psychodynamic (21.9%), eclectic (19.8%), humanistic/experiential (4.4%), family systems (3.9%), and other (4.6%). That being said, a number of clinicians who regard themselves as delivering CBT may overrate their competency in this approach to therapy (Brosan, Reynolds, & Moore, 2007, 2008) and, from patient report, often do not deliver the key elements of CBT (Stobie, Taylor, Quigley, Ewing, & Salkovskis, 2007). These deficiencies may be due to inadequate training in CBT. Programs in psychiatry, psychology, and social work across the United States were surveyed to establish the adequacy of training in empirically based psychotherapies, the latter being comprised mostly of CBT (Weissman et al., 2006). Only 17.8% of training programs provided both didactic and clinical supervision training in empirically based treatments. Interestingly, the highest rates of adequate training were in psychiatry, possibly because of the inclusion of CBT in accreditation criteria for psychiatry residency programs. Such requirements do not exist for psychology or social work programs. Lack of CBT competency, even among self-described CBT clinicians, may be additionally attributed to the overemphasis on training in CBT *procedures* at the cost of training in CBT *principles*. This imbalance may stem in part from the manualization of CBT interventions for various problems. Whereas manualization is a positive feature that facilitates empirical evaluation of CBT and enhances CBT dissemination, it may have inadvertently encouraged too much focus on procedure over principle. A good understanding of the principles underlying CBT, an exposition of which is a primary goal of this book, is necessary for optimal tailoring of CBT procedures to each presenting problem.

Nevertheless, even in the hands of less experienced therapists, CBT is a highly effective approach, in addition to being noted for the best evidence of all psychotherapeutic treatments (Roth & Fonagy, 1996). As such, CBT is entirely consistent with the evidence-based practice movement being encouraged by the American Psychological Association (APA; 2005). Evidence-based practice principles encourage clinicians to combine their clinical expertise with available research evidence for treatment planning. To facilitate the dissemination of evidence-based principles, the Division 12 (APA) Task Force on Promotion and Dissemination of Psychological Procedures (1995), updated by Chambless and Ollendick in 2001, and the Task Force on Effective Psychosocial Interventions: A Lifespan Perspective (Spirito, 1999) have published information about treatments that work for particular problems. The majority of empirically supported treatments that are cited in these documents are cognitive therapies, behavioral therapies, and cognitive and behavioral therapies, jointly termed CBT herein.

2

History

The history of cognitive–behavioral therapy (CBT) began with a heavily behavioral orientation throughout the 1950s to 1970s. The growth in cognitive therapy in the 1960s was followed by the integration of cognitive and behavioral approaches in the 1980s and onward. A third wave of behavioral therapies is now emerging, one which de-emphasizes the content approach to cognition and instead emphasizes the function of cognition.

ORIGINS

As a backlash to the prevailing "non-scientific" psychoanalytical approaches to treatment in the first half of the 20th century, the principles of learning theory guided a new, science-based approach to the conceptualization, assessment, and treatment of mental disorders. This new approach was behavior therapy. As noted by Levis (1999),

> the behavioral therapy movement identified itself with the experimental field of learning, which already had an existing data base, a common language structure, and a guiding philosophy of science. By stressing the importance of defining terms and procedures operationally, coupled

with a strong commitment to assessment and research, those involved hoped to reduce the existing chaos in the mental health field by developing new treatment techniques and assessment procedures based on established and documented principles of learning and behavior. (p. 157)

Two sets of learning theory principles guided the behavior therapy movement in its original form: classical (or respondent) conditioning and instrumental (or operant) conditioning. Briefly, classical conditioning (most associated with Pavlov, 1927) is based on environmental stimuli that produce reflexive responses, such as when a physical threat from another person produces a reflexive fear response. Hence, an innately evocative stimulus (or an unconditional stimulus, US) produces an unconditional, reflexive response (UR). Furthermore, if repeatedly paired with the US, a previously neutral stimulus can become a conditional stimulus (CS) that evokes a conditional response (CR) similar to the original UR. For example, as a result of the aversive experience of a motor vehicle accident (US) and the fear and pain it produced (UR), motor vehicles (CS) may become a signal for potential future accidents and therefore evoke a conditional anxiety response. Consequently, anxiety becomes conditioned to motor vehicles and may even be evoked *automatically*, or without conscious appraisal of perceived danger. In classical conditioning theory, the history of learned associations between neutral and innately evocative stimuli is presumed to explain current emotional–behavioral responses. Classical conditioning was and continues to be evoked as an explanatory process in the psychopathology and treatment of emotional disorders (e.g., anxiety disorders) as well as substance use related disorders and certain sexual disorders, among others.

Instrumental conditioning, originated by Thorndike (1898) and extended by Skinner (1938), refers to the modification of the occurrence or form of behavior by its consequences. As such, it is relevant to voluntary rather than reflexive behaviors. That is, a response is "selected"—and is thus voluntary—based on the consequences likely to be received; operant behavior "operates" on the environment and is maintained by its consequences. An example is the increased frequency of drug consumption due to the reinforcing, albeit temporary, euphoria produced by a substance and/or by the relief a substance provides from other negative emotions. The reinforcement provided by the euphoria and/or the escape from unpleasant emotions increases the likelihood of engaging in drug consumption in the future. In instrumental conditioning, behavioral responses are selected and shaped by the entire array of positive and negative consequences that the behavior produces. Operant conditioning has been applied to a wide range of disordered behavior, such as substance use related disorders, externalizing behaviors, pain management, and aspects of psychosis.

The course by which these two learning theories were translated into treatments differed. Pavlov and colleagues did not consider the treatment implications of classical conditioning. In fact, the first applications were made by Watson and Rayner (1920), who demonstrated the conditioning of a fear reaction in young "Albert," and by Mary Cover Jones (1924), who developed fear reduction techniques for children based on learning theory. However, neither their work nor the work of Pavlov and his colleagues had any impact on clinical practice at the time, possibly because therapy was the domain of psychiatry that was dominated by psychoanalytic theory (Eelen & Vervliet, 2006). However, following World War II (i.e., 1945), there was an increased demand for therapeutic interventions and therapists, and the time was ripe for psychologists to receive training in new methods of intervention. This cause was met by the work of Joseph Wolpe, in South Africa, who had become dissatisfied with psychoanalytical approaches. Wolpe was interested in the experimental foundations of learning and their application to neuroses, out of which he developed systematic desensitization for treating fears and anxiety disorders (Wolpe, 1958).

Wolpe began by reviewing Pavlov's research (1927) and Hull's (1943) learning theory (which stated that behavior is influenced by drives and incentives, and conditioning only occurs if a reinforcement satisfies a need). Then he investigated the principles of aversive classical conditioning in cats. Once he established that cats became fearful of their cages by shocking the floor of the cage, Wolpe next established that he could eventually extinguish their aversively conditioned fears by a procedure of counterconditioning. In this procedure, the drive for hunger and food became a means for reciprocally inhibiting the fear response. That is, the cats were mildly food deprived, and then food was placed at progressively closer distances to the cage. The hunger and drive for food overcame the anxiety, and the cats eventually reentered the cages. Next, he extended his investigation to human fears and phobias. In an extensive series of case studies, Wolpe (1958) demonstrated the positive effects of graduated imaginal exposure to fear-producing situations, using the relaxation response (via progressive muscle relaxation, developed by Jacobson, 1938), as a counterconditioner of the anxiety associated with each image. This method was named systematic desensitization, and hence was born the first tested, standardized, and replicable method of behavioral intervention for emotional disorders.

In contrast to Pavlov's lack of involvement in treatment application, Skinner directly contributed to the translation of instrumental conditioning principles to treatment interventions. He spearheaded the development of behavioral interventions in the United States in the 1950s and 1960s (e.g., Lindsley, Skinner, & Solomon, 1953), a development that also was spurred by the needs following World War II. Skinner believed that the solid body of scientific knowledge regarding the behavior of organisms provided alternative solutions to psychoanalytic approaches to treatment. He described the new form of treatment in his book *Science and Human Behavior* (1953). For him, treatment involved introducing observable variables to compensate for and correct a history that had produced "unfavorable" behaviors. That is, treatments based on instrumental learning, later coined *behavior modification*, involved basic principles of extinction of undesirable behaviors and reshaping by reinforcement of newly emitted and desirable behaviors, on varying schedules of reinforcement. Skinner and Lindsley first implemented instrumental principles for the management of problem behaviors (e.g., self-injurious) in patients with psychosis at the Metropolitan State Hospital, Massachusetts. Then, these behavioral modification procedures were extended to aspects of autism and other problem behaviors associated with mental retardation. "Simply stated, hospital wards were regarded and treated as huge Skinner boxes, in which the environmental events surrounding the emission of behavior by clients were controlled so as to extinguish or shape desired responses" (Goldfried & Davison, 1994, p. 5).

Although differing in principles, classical and instrumental behavioral approaches shared several features in common. Specifically, both approaches viewed "disorders" as the result of faulty learning. They held that because abnormal behavior is governed by the same principles that govern normal behavior, most abnormal behavior can be modified by behavioral procedures (Rachman & Wilson, 1980). Another shared feature was the reliance on empirical methods and principles and the motivation to move the field forward by not relying on nonmeasurable (i.e., psychoanalytic) constructs. The commitment to an applied science approach meant reliance on an explicit testable conceptual framework; therapeutic techniques that could be described with sufficient precision to be measured and replicated; experimental evaluation of treatment methods and concepts to determine their effects; and emphasis on rigorous evaluation of specific methods applied to particular problems rather than global assessments of ill-defined procedures applied to heterogeneous problems (Rachman & Wilson, 1980).

In the 1950s, the acceptance of behavioral theories and therapies was greatly influenced by Hans Eysenck, who was given the task of constructing a training program for clinical psychologists at the Maudsley Institute in London, the leading center for training in the United Kingdom. Eysenck himself was strongly influenced by the view that psychoanalysis was unfalsifiable and therefore nonscientific. He began by reviewing the efficacy of existing psychotherapy methods and, in an influential paper (Eysenck, 1952), concluded that traditional (psychoanalytical) therapies were no more effective than the passage of time or placebo. In 1960, he published the book *Behavior Therapy and the Neuroses*, in which he concluded that the only effective therapy was one based on modern learning theory, such as systematic desensitization and instrumental procedures, including aversion therapy. Thus, Eysenck instituted a model of clinical training at the Maudsley Institute that was guided by scientific behavioral psychology, a model that was subsequently reinforced by Stanley Rachman and Isaac Marks and thereafter continued to influence clinical psychology training in the United Kingdom. Furthermore, in 1963, Eysenck founded the journal *Behaviour Research and Therapy*, which provided an outlet for the results of ongoing investigations of behavioral therapies and thereby contributed significantly to their dissemination worldwide.

There was a burgeoning of efficacy studies of behavioral treatments in the 1970s and 1980s. Simultaneously, a set of standards for evaluating therapeutic outcomes, such as treatment credibility, treatment integrity, and rigorous control comparisons, was developed. However, as interest in efficacy outcomes and the technology of behavioral treatments increased, interest in the "theory" underlying those treatments and the "theoretical cohesion" of classical and operant conditioning principles waned. According to Levis (1999), "the term behavioral therapist, which formerly signified an individual committed to a behavioral philosophy of science, soon lost any meaningful operational specificity" (p. 159). Others similarly noted that behavioral therapy became divorced from behavioral theory (e.g., Eifert, Forsyth, & Schauss, 1993).

Independently, concern began to be expressed about the adequacy of learning theory accounts of psychopathology (e.g., Bandura, 1978). For example, the classical conditioning model of fears and phobias was criticized for its inability to explain why not all individuals who undergo an aversive experience develop a phobia. At the same time, operant principles began to be viewed as overly simplistic and mechanistic, to the point that "clinicians were frustrated with radical behaviorists' failure to account for language and thought processes in terms useful for clinicians" (Eifert et al., 1993, p. 108). Furthermore, clinicians were dissatisfied with the results of behavioral treatment for depression and were in search of another model, something they found in cognitive therapy.

The pioneers of cognitive therapy were Albert Ellis (1957), who developed a cognitive therapy coined rational–emotive behavior therapy; Aaron Beck (1963), whose approach is called cognitive therapy; and Donald Meichenbaum (1977), who developed self-instruction training. In brief, Ellis viewed irrational thinking as the source of problem behaviors and emotions and emphasized direct disputation of irrational thinking and the development of rational thinking as the mode of treatment. Beck's approach emphasizes surface level distortions in information processing and their relationships with underlying or core maladaptive belief systems; instead of disputation as a therapeutic technique, this approach uses Socratic questioning to help individuals see the errors in their thinking and generate alternative, more evidence-based appraisals. Meichenbaum's approach teaches a method of self-instruction for facing challenging situations. Despite the differences in their cognitive approaches, all three viewed *disorders* as arising from faulty thinking; they agreed that dysfunctional thinking generates and maintains symptoms of psychopathology and that the content of cognition is the primary determinant of behavior and emotions. In marked contrast to the strictly behavioral approach, the cognitive approach addressed "nonmeasurable" cognitive concepts. However, the cognitive approach differed from inferential psychoanalytical approaches by focusing on present problems and present thinking and by regarding verbalizations as valid data points rather than as symbols of unconscious processes.

Paradigmatic shifts simultaneously were occurring in classical and instrumental conditioning theories. In the newer models, cognition was accommodated within learning theory models not just as a response but as a factor possessing causal significance or as a mediator of conditioning (e.g., Rescorla, 1968). Debate over the role of implicit or nonconscious expectancies versus explicit conscious appraisals in instrumental and classical conditioning continues. Nonetheless, the molding of cognition into conditioning was yet another factor that facilitated the uptake of cognitive theories and their blending into behavioral theories and therapies.

Bandura's (1973) social learning theory, in which cognitive processes were assigned a role as critical determinants of behavior, was another positive influence on the acceptance of cognitions as a target for therapy. Bandura established that learning is not solely dependent on direct experience but occurs through judgments as well (although direct experience was still regarded as a critical determinant in its own right). Hence, in his model of reciprocal determinism, behaviors, cognitions, and environmental factors are viewed as continuously reinforcing each other. Subsequently, Bandura (1977) emphasized a particular cognitive construct, coined self-efficacy, as a primary determinant of behavioral change and as the primary mechanism underlying therapeutic interventions. Bandura posited that self-efficacy was more effectively raised through performance accomplishment rather than by verbal persuasion. This may be one of several reasons why his model was never fully incorporated into cognitive theories and therapies, although it was incorporated as a mediator of behavioral treatments.

Yet one more factor that facilitated the transition from behaviorism to cognitive–behaviorism was the value given by the cognitive approach to behavioral techniques, albeit as a means for changing maladaptive thinking styles. Thus, behaviorists did not have to relinquish their behavioral technology as they extended their targets beyond overt behavior to the domain of cognition. By the early 1980s, the cognitive revolution was fully underway. The establishment of centers, such as Ellis's Centers for Rational Emotive Behavior Therapy, and the publication of treatment manuals, such as the *Cognitive Therapy of Depression* (1979) by Beck and colleagues, paved the way for clinical efficacy studies and dissemination of cognitive therapy procedures to clinicians at large.

The development of behavior therapy and cognitive therapy followed very different pathways. Behavior therapy developed out of experimental principles of learning theory and experimentation that were first tested in laboratory studies in animals, followed by laboratory studies in humans, and finally therapy outcome studies with clinical samples. Wolpe epitomized this approach in his studies of classical conditioning and reciprocal inhibition. In contrast, cognitive therapy derived from astute clinical observation by Ellis, Beck, and Meichenbaum of the role patients' self-statements and beliefs played in their emotional and behavioral.responding. Curiously, a science of cognitive psychology was growing at around the same time as cognitive therapy, but the two cognitive fields developed almost in isolation of each other. It was not until the mid to late 1990s that integrationist efforts were made, wherein theoretical principles and therapeutic procedures of cognitive therapy began to be judged in light of the principles and empirical findings from the science of cognitive psychology.

CONTEMPORARY APPROACH
AND EVOLUTION TO PRESENT

The merging of behavioral and cognitive therapies resulted in therapists paying more attention to clients' expectations and understandings as valid data points in their own right, therefore "supplying the content to behavior therapy" (Rachman, 1997, p. 18). The focus on cognitive content is achieved within the context of helping clients to become aware of maladaptive cognitive–affective–behavioral chains and to create learning experiences and acquire coping skills for interrupting those maladaptive sequences and for producing more adaptive responses.

More specifically, contemporary CBT typically begins with an individually based functional analysis of problem behaviors, cognitions, and emotions and the reciprocal interactions among them that serve to trigger and maintain maladaptive responding (i.e., causal modeling). In contrast to functional analysis as originally specified in instrumentally based behavioral modification procedures, contemporary CBT takes a broader view by considering the antecedents and consequences of behaviors, identification of which stimuli are eliciting which CRs, and the cognitions that are influencing behaviors and emotions. A functional analysis also evaluates the role of cultural factors in the expression and causal modeling of problem behaviors, cognitions, and emotions. The method of functional analysis is first implemented through the therapist's questioning and observations, sometimes extending to behavioral observations of clients in their natural environment. It is then transferred to clients who are taught to adopt a personal scientist perspective, in which they become observers of their own patterns of behavioral, cognitive, and emotional responding in given environmental and cultural contexts. The functional analysis then guides the treatment plan.

Next, a set of change-oriented strategies are implemented. These may include the identification of idiosyncratic errors in conscious appraisals and their links with underlying core beliefs. A set of skills, often termed cognitive restructuring, is taught for modifying distorted appraisals and core beliefs, through disputation and logical empiricism. Behavioral methodologies are incorporated through behavioral experimentation, also called hypothesis testing, designed to collect evidence that disconfirms distorted thinking. Another set of intervention strategies address classically conditioned responses. An example would be systematic and repeated exposure to irrationally feared objects to extinguish CRs. Combining the cognitive and behavioral principles and procedures, changes in implicit cognitions as a result of the exposure experience are accompanied by explicit reappraisals that aversive outcomes do not occur and/or are not as aversive as anticipated.

Yet another set of strategies replaces maladaptive behaviors with adaptive behaviors through shaping and scheduled reinforcers and punishers. An example would be engaging in positively reinforcing activities as a means for correcting the low rate of positive reinforcement that characterizes depression. Again, these activities may be accompanied by explicit reappraisals of the value of the positive reinforcement, to offset cognitive biases that devalue positive reinforcers. The relative emphasis given to the principles and skills of cognitive restructuring versus operant and respondent learning varies according to each clinician's leaning toward more cognitive versus more behavioral approaches to cognitive–behavioral change and, of course, the nature of the presenting problem. However, the truly integrated cognitive–behavioral clinician gives credence to both. The treatment plan is continuously revised in accordance with ongoing evaluation of the target emotions, behaviors, and cognitions. The final step of treatment is a relapse prevention plan, designed to maintain the skills that have been acquired over time.

As noted previously, CBT is widely used and is the most commonly cited therapy orientation among randomly surveyed clinicians from the American Psychological Association (Stewart & Chambless, 2007). Part of its popularity is attributable to the empirical support that CBT has achieved, showing positive results for a large array of psychosocial problems. As the most commonly cited empirically supported treatment, the scope and demonstrated utility of CBT are attractive to training programs and practitioners in general practice. The level of empirical support is a function of the empirical philosophy that is the essence of CBT.

The popularity of CBT is enhanced by a feature of empirical methodology, which is manualization of intervention procedures. Manualization was a necessary step for empirical evaluation, since manualization allows for replicability of CBT in independently conducted studies. While there may be some downsides to strict manualization, such as failures to tailor CBT to the presenting problem and perhaps failure to fully learn and appreciate the principles underlying CBT, manualization has played a major role in the dissemination of CBT in training programs and clinical practice in general. Furthermore, the popularity of CBT is consistent with the current emphasis upon evidence-based medicine. Finally, the time-limited nature of CBT and its suitability for delivery in group formats adds more to its cache by virtue of cost effectiveness, which of course is of high importance in the world of managed care.

FUTURE DIRECTIONS

We are now on the verge of yet another turning of the tides in the trajectory of CBT. As cognitive theories and therapies developed, cognitive processes began to be conceptualized much like processes of a computer. In this model, cognition is comprised of a number of processes, such as encoding, retrieval, attributional and appraisal. This type of theorizing placed cognitive therapy in line, to a certain degree, with the science of cognitive psychology (i.e., the science of ways in which information is attended to, stored, and retrieved). Hence, from the 1990s onward, attention has been given to the ways in which the science of cognitive psychology informs cognitive and behavioral therapies. Indeed, advances in our scientific understanding of the cognition–emotion interface for emotional disorders support some of the premises of cognitive therapies. However, at its core, cognitive therapy remains a therapy that targets the conscious content of cognition. The science of cognitive psychology has brought to light certain limitations of a content-based cognitive model of psychopathology and therapy. For example, it is now well recognized that the majority of information processing occurs at subconscious levels, without conscious appraisal. The adequacy of attempts to change subconscious cognition through conscious reappraisals has been questioned (e.g., Teasdale & Barnard, 1993). Alternative methods for shifting styles of information processing that do not depend on conscious appraisals are now being tested as complements to or replacements for cognitive therapy. These include mindfulness and acceptance-based approaches, which have been coined the third wave of behavioral therapies (Hayes, 2008). In some of these newer treatment models, such as mindfulness-based cognitive therapy (e.g., Williams et al., 2008), direct attempts to change the content of conscious appraisals is accompanied by skills of mindfulness. In other models, such as acceptance and commitment therapy (Hayes, Strosahl, & Wilson, 1999), the role of conscious appraisal is not ignored, but instead of directly addressing the content of those appraisals, attention is given to their function and ways of disrupting that function.

Another recent development that is proving a challenge for more purely cognitive approaches is the evidence pertaining to newer behavioral treatments for depression. Dissatisfaction with behavioral approaches for depression was a major impetus for the development of cognitive therapies. However, in a complete "reversal of fortune," the effectiveness of behavioral activation treatment for depression has been gaining support. This treatment is based on principles of operant conditioning and reinforcement (Jacobson, Martell, & Dimidjian, 2001). Moreover, behavioral activation may be superior to cognitive therapies for severe depression (Dimidjian et al., 2006). Along with this upsurge in operant learning behavioral principles of therapy is a reinvigorated interest in classical conditioning principles of exposure therapy for anxiety disorders, spurred by advances in the basic science of learning and memory (e.g., Craske et al., 2008). In sum, the third wave of CBT is both shifting back to behavioral principles and extending forward to mindfulness and acceptance.

3

Theory

The principles and theories that underlie cognitive–behavioral therapy (CBT) derive from several different sources that have become interweaved with each other as CBT has developed from its initial behavioral routes to the contemporary cognitive–behavioral integration. After presenting the overarching goals of CBT, this chapter outlines the ways in which each set of theoretical principles conceptualizes maladaptive behaviors, emotions, and cognitions and their modification. First is learning theory, including classical conditioning and instrumental conditioning principles. Next is social learning theory, which provides a cognitive theory for behavioral change. Finally, cognitive appraisal theory is presented. Ways in which these theories overlap and accommodate each other are described. As previously noted, the more behaviorally oriented clinician will draw mainly from learning theory in conceptualizing a presenting problem and formulating a treatment plan, whereas the more cognitively oriented clinician will favor the theory and principles of cognitive appraisal. The cognitive–behavioral clinician can comfortably draw from both learning theories (including social learning theory) and cognitive appraisal theory to conceptualize a problem and formulate a treatment plan.

GOALS

Broadly speaking, the goal of CBT is to achieve symptom reduction and improvement in quality of life through the replacement of maladaptive emotional, behavioral, and cognitive response chains with more adaptive responses. Underlying this goal is the notion that problem behaviors, cognitions, and emotions have been acquired at least in part through experience and learning and therefore are open to modification through new experience and learning.[1] The target of CBT is to teach new ways of responding and to develop new learning experiences that together promote more adaptive patterns of behavioral, affective, and cognitive responding. Also, these changes are attempted within relatively brief periods of time; in other words, CBT aims to be not only problem-focused but also time limited.

Another goal of CBT is for long-term positive effects that are self-maintaining. Thus, learning experiences are repeated, and new ways of responding are practiced over a sufficient number of occasions and contexts that they become the major determinants and preferred methods of responding in the long term, independent of the therapy context. In this way, CBT aims to tool clients with their own repertoire of skills for dealing with problematic situations and thereby become less and less dependent on, and eventually autonomous from, the therapist.

These two overarching goals are achieved within the framework of a set of guiding principles of behavioral theory and science and cognitive theory (and more recently, cognitive science) for conceptualizing presenting problems and formulating intervention strategies. These principles drive another goal, which is to use an individually based functional analysis of the causal relations among cognitions, behaviors, emotions, and environmental and cultural contexts for tailoring intervention strategies specifically to the needs of a given problem. Thus, rather than assuming that one standard treatment fits all, CBT is based on careful observation and understanding of each individual's presenting problem. Functional analysis refers to an analysis of not only the instrumental antecedents and consequences, but

---

[1] Genetic endowments and temperament are viewed as additional contributing factors to problem behaviors, cognitions, and emotions.

also which stimuli are producing which conditional responses (CRs), which cognitions are contributing to behaviors and emotions, and within which environmental and cultural contexts these occur. The therapist and client then make an informed choice about which methods for behavioral and cognitive change to use from a variety of different intervention strategies.

Another goal is to have a flexible approach to implementation, which is facilitated by ongoing evaluation and modification of intervention strategies as appropriate. Linked with this is the aim of engaging the client in the process of experimentation and ongoing evaluation of the effectiveness of the chosen interventions. Evaluation not only permits revision to the intervention strategies where necessary but provides an assessment of overall progress. Overall progress is measured by agreed-upon markers between the client and the therapist, and when the evidence indicates lack of progress, consideration is given to alternative treatment methods. Clearly, this entails therapist–client collaboration in formulating and implementing a treatment plan and a highly active orientation on the part of the client.

KEY CONCEPTS

This section is divided into key concepts of learning theory (classical and instrumental conditioning), social learning theory, and cognitive appraisal theory. The ways in which these theories overlap and accommodate each other are described as well.

Learning Theory: Classical Conditioning

Classical (or respondent) conditioning depends on innately evocative stimuli (US) producing an unconditional, reflexive response (UR), such as when physical injury reflexively produces a pain grimace. When a neutral stimulus is paired with the US, the neutral stimulus becomes a conditional stimulus (CS) with powers to elicit a CR that resembles the original UR (Pavlov, 1927). For example, in the case of persons undergoing chemotherapy (US) that causes them to vomit (UR), the nurse may become a CS by association with administration of the chemotherapy. Consequently, sight of the nurse may produce conditional nausea in the patient even before the chemotherapy is administered the next time. Furthermore, through a process of generalization, the CR may begin to emerge in reaction to stimuli similar to the original CS. Following from the preceding example, generalization may result in conditional nausea in response to seeing the medical clinic or administrative staff. In addition, Pavlov (1927) demonstrated that if the CS is presented enough times without the US, the CR lessens or extinguishes. Continuing the example, once the chemotherapy course has completed, repeated visits to the clinic for checkups would result in an eventual diminution of the conditional nausea response.

The principles of aversive classical conditioning are applied mostly to anxiety disorders. Early theorizing of fears and phobias relied on *contiguous* classical conditioning models in which a neutral stimulus develops conditional fear-provoking properties simply by virtue of close temporal pairing with an aversive stimulus. Examples would include ridicule and rejection by a peer group leading to conditional fear (i.e., phobia) of social situations or barking by a ferocious dog leading to phobias of dogs. These early theories were criticized for being too simplistic (e.g., Rachman, 1978), especially as not everyone who undergoes an aversive experience develops a phobia. That is, not everyone who is ridiculed by a peer group develops social phobia, and not everyone who is barked at by a ferocious dog develops a phobia of dogs. Recent revisions to classical conditioning models of fear and anxiety (see Mineka & Zinbarg, 2006, for a review) correct the earlier pitfalls.

The newer models continue to emphasize the role of aversive experiences in the formation of conditional anxiety responses, but instead of being limited to direct experience with negative events, they extend to conditioning through vicarious observation of negative events or even informational transmission about negative events (see Mineka & Zinbarg, 2006, for citations of supportive research). For example, observing someone else be physically injured and/or be terrified in a car accident may be sufficient for the development of a conditional fear of motor vehicles, as would being told about the dangers of driving and the high likelihood of fatal car accidents. Vicarious and informational transmission of conditioning represents the incorporation of cognitive processes into classical conditioning models. The newer conditioning models also recognize that a myriad of constitutional, contextual, and post-event factors moderate the likelihood of developing a conditional phobia after an aversive event.

Constitutional factors (or individual difference variables) include temperament. For example, individuals who tend to be more nervous in general are believed to be more likely to develop a conditional phobia after a negative experience than less "neurotic" individuals who undergo the same negative experience. Another constitutional factor is personal history of experience with the stimulus that is subsequently paired with an aversive event, as prior positive experience may buffer against the development of a conditional phobia. For example, the effects of observing one parent react fearfully to heights may be buffered by having previously observed other family members react without fear to heights. Recognition of individual difference factors addresses the earlier criticism that not everyone who undergoes an aversive experience develops a phobia; rather, certain individuals are prone to developing conditional phobic responses following an aversive experience as a function of their temperament and life experience.

Contextual factors at the time of the aversive experience include intensity and controllability: More intense and less controllable negative events are more likely to generate conditional fear than less intense and/or more controllable negative events. According to these premises, individuals trapped for a lengthy period of time inside an elevator stuck between floors would be more likely to develop a conditional fear of elevators than the person who can escape from a stuck elevator relatively quickly. Similarly, soldiers at the front line of combat would be more likely to develop conditional fear than those further away. Another contextual factor pertains to principles of preparedness, or the innate propensity to rapidly acquire conditional fear of stimuli that posed threat to our early ancestors (Seligman, 1971). Examples of such stimuli are heights, closed-in spaces from which it is difficult to escape, reptiles, and signals of rejection from one's group. Thus, as a species, humans are more likely to develop long-lasting conditional fears following negative experiences in prepared situations (e.g., being laughed at by peers) compared to other, "nonprepared" situations (e.g., being shocked by an electric outlet). Preparedness is believed to account for the nonrandomness of phobias, or the fact that some objects or situations are much more likely to become feared than other objects.

Following conditioning, a variety of postevent processes may influence the persistence of conditional fear, including additional aversive experiences, expectancies for aversive outcomes (Davey, 2006), and avoidant responding. For example, the child who is teased by a peer group, then ruminates about being teased, expects further teasing, and avoids the peer group is more likely to develop social anxiety than the child who undergoes the same teasing but returns to the peer group the next day. In sum, recent models of classical conditioning recognize that the development of an excessive and chronic conditional fear is not explained by a specific aversive event in isolation but by an interaction among predisposing features, the aversive event, and reactions to the event.

The classical conditioning model is also applicable to disorders related to substance use, in which the principles of appetitive conditioning apply as well as aversive conditioning. Appetitive conditioning refers to conditioning with a US that produces an innately positive response, whereas aversive conditioning refers to conditioning with a US that produces an innately negative response. In the case of substance use disorders, euphoria serves as an innately positive UR to the drug. Over time, environmental stimuli present during the euphoric state become conditional. These environmental stimuli may be the locations in which the drugs are usually consumed or the people with whom drug taking normally occurs. Consequently, the environmental stimuli elicit conditional urges or cravings to take more of the drug. Known as the *conditioned appetitive motivational model of craving* (Stewart, deWit, & Eikelboom, 1984), this model explains the difficulties experienced when recovering drug users return to the environments in which they originally developed their drug dependence. That is, just seeing a group of friends with whom drugs used to be taken may be enough to produce cravings for the drugs, even though the drugs themselves are not present.

Siegel (1978) proposed the conditional compensatory response model, a classical conditioning model of drug tolerance. In this model, environmental stimuli associated with drug intake become associated with the drug's effect on the body and elicit a CR that is opposite to the effect of the drug, driven by an automatic drive for body homeostasis. As this CR increases in magnitude with continued drug use, the drug's effects decrease and tolerance increases. Finally, aversive classical conditioning has been evoked as an additional mechanism by which stimuli associated with the unpleasant periods of drug withdrawal elicit withdrawal-like symptoms. For example, if withdrawal is typically experienced upon waking from sleep, then waking may elicit conditioned withdrawal symptoms that in turn could drive continued drug use to minimize withdrawal effects.

Principles of Treatment

The treatment model that derives from classical conditioning states that behaviors and emotions can be changed by disrupting the associations that have formed between a cue (CS) and either an aversive or a pleasant outcome (US). In learning theory, this is referred to as *extinction*. Conditioning involves pairings of the CS with the US; extinction involves repeated presentations of the CS without the US. The corresponding treatment is referred to as exposure therapy; in this therapy, the client repeatedly faces the object of fear (in the case of anxiety disorders) or the drug-related cue (in the case of substance use disorders) in the absence of an aversive or a pleasant outcome. As an example, individuals with social anxiety would be encouraged to repeatedly enter social situations without being ridiculed or rejected, or individuals with posttraumatic stress disorder would be encouraged to repeatedly enter places where they were previously traumatized without being retraumatized. As another example, individuals who drink alcohol excessively would be exposed to substance cues (e.g., sight or smell of alcohol) and prevented from consuming the alcohol so that the CS is repeatedly presented in the absence of reinforcement that comes from the consumption of the drug. This is called cue exposure.

Several mechanisms are believed to underlie extinction and thereby exposure therapy. One such mechanism is habituation (or decreased response strength simply as a function of repeated exposure). Another mechanism, inhibitory learning, is considered to be even more central to extinction (Myers & Davis, 2007). Inhibitory learning means that the original association between a CS and aversive event is not erased throughout extinction, but rather a new inhibitory association (or expectancy) is developed. For example, as a result of exposure therapy for fear of dogs, an original "excitatory" association between a dog and ferocious barking would be complemented by a new "inhibitory" association between a dog and the absence of ferocious barking. Consequently, as a result of exposure therapy, two sets of associations exist in memory. Once exposure therapy is over, the level of fear that is expressed when a dog is encountered in daily life will depend on which set of associations is evoked. Interestingly, basic research by Bouton and colleagues (reviewed in Bouton, Woods, Moody, Sunsay, & Garcia-Gutierrez, 2006) indicates that context is important in determining which set of associations is evoked. If the previously feared stimulus is encountered in a context that is similar to the extinction/exposure therapy context, then the inhibitory association will be more likely to be activated, resulting in minimal fear. However, if the previously feared stimulus is encountered in a context distinctly different from the extinction/exposure therapy context, then the original excitatory association is more likely to be activated, resulting in more fear. Following the example of dog phobia, assume that the exposure treatment was conducted in a dog training center. Then, once treatment is over, a dog is encountered on a neighborhood sidewalk, a context that is distinctly different from the dog training center. On the sidewalk, the original excitatory fear association is more likely to be activated than the new inhibitory association that was developed throughout exposure treatment, resulting in the expression of fear.

Thus, a change in context is presumed to at least partially account for the return of fear that sometimes occurs following exposure therapy for anxiety disorders (Craske et al., 2008) and relapse following treatment for substance use disorders (e.g., Collins & Brandon, 2002). In addition to context, other factors can also reactivate the original excitatory association. One such factor is being exposed to a new negative experience. Thus, persons who are successfully treated for their fear of dogs may have their fear return if they are subsequently involved in a car accident (in learning theory this is called *reinstatement*) or if they are barked at by another ferocious dog (termed *reacquisition*).

Innovative strategies are now being tested for enhancing new inhibitory associations throughout exposure therapy (see Craske et al., 2008, for a review). In addition, attention is being given to ways of enhancing the retrievability of new inhibitory associations once exposure therapy is completed, and thereby decreasing relapse, such as conducting exposure therapy in multiple contexts. Another is to provide retrieval cues that remind clients, when they are outside of the therapy context, of the new learning that took place in the therapy context or at least recommend to clients that they actively try to remember what they learned when in the therapy context (see Craske et al., 2008).

Another key concept associated with extinction of CRs is safety signals, or conditional inhibitors that predict the absence of the aversive stimulus. When the conditional inhibitor is present, the CS is not paired with the US; when the conditional inhibitor is not present, the CS is paired with the US. In the experimental literature, safety signals alleviate distress to the CS in the short term, but when no longer present, fear to the CS returns (Lovibond, Davis, & O'Flaherty, 2000). Common safety signals for anxiety disorder clients are the presence of another person, therapists, medications, food, or drink. Thus, clients with panic disorder and agoraphobia may feel relatively comfortable walking around a shopping mall with a bottle of medications in their pocket (even if the medications are never taken) but report being anxious in the shopping mall when without the bottle of medication. Conditional inhibitors have been shown to interfere with extinction learning in human experimental studies (e.g., Lovibond et al., 2000).

Also, several studies have evaluated safety signals in phobic samples (see Craske et al., 2008, for a review). For example, claustrophobic participants who are encouraged to use safety signals during exposure to being inside a small booth report more fear at later testing to the claustrophobic booth without the safety signals than those who complete exposure without safety signals. (The safety signals were to open a window on the side of the booth and to check that the booth door unlocked.) Just the perception of safety (i.e., knowing that the safety signals were available even though they were not used) has the same detrimental effects on outcome as the actual use of safety signals. Thus, exposure therapy typically proceeds by not only having clients repeatedly face their feared objects or situations, but at the same time being weaned from typical safety signals.

Role of Cognitive Variables in Classical Conditioning

In its earliest form, classical conditioning was construed as largely mechanistic and reflexive, with little room for the role of cognition. However, the model has evolved over time to incorporate cognitive factors. The "cognitive revolution" can be attributed to researchers such as Tolman

(1948), who challenged purely mechanistic models, and Rescorla (1968), who established that conditioning involves the acquisition of information, so that CRs are elicited when the CS predicts that the US is likely to occur and are inhibited when it predicts that the US is less likely to occur. Contemporary models generally dictate that the CS activates a memory representation of the US and an expectation of its occurrence (see Kirsch, Lynn, Vigorito, & Miller, 2004, for a review). An expectancy is a future-oriented belief.

Expectancies may be implicit (automatic) or explicit (conscious), and debate continues as to the necessity of explicit expectancies in conditioning (Kirsch et al., 2004). The more mechanistic view dictates that while explicit expectancies may be produced by conditioning trials, they are not necessary for conditioning. In support, conditioning can occur to a CS that is not consciously perceived, and when the relationship between a CS and US is unknown, at least with "prepared" CSs (see Ohman & Mineka, 2001). The alternative point of view dictates that explicit expectancies mediate the effects of conditioning and cause the CR. In support, simply informing participants about a relationship between a CS and US can produce a CR (previously referred to as informational transmission), just as instruction alone can produce extinction of a CR. In addition, strength of the CR varies as a function of information about the intensity of the US (Kirsch et al., 2004). Hence, CRs may develop through either mechanistic/automatic or higher-order cognitive processes (e.g., Ohman & Mineka, 2001).

Recognition of the role of cognitive factors in classical conditioning provided a pathway through which cognitive theories could be intertwined with learning theories. For example, an abundance of evidence points to biases in the expectancies of individuals with anxiety disorders, including overattention to negative stimuli, overestimation of the likelihood of negative events, and catastrophizing the meaning of negative events (see Davey, 2006). Hence, the anxious person may hold particularly high expectancies for an intensely aversive experience, which in turn contributes to the acquisition of conditional responding and/or interferes with its extinction (Davey, 2006). In other words, maladaptive assumptions and beliefs may contribute to the perceived intensity of the US and/or the perceived likelihood of its reoccurrence, which in turn mediates stronger conditioning. Furthermore, correction of these expectancy biases, as would be achieved through cognitive therapy, can be easily incorporated into exposure therapy as a means of enhancing extinction of CRs. That is, cognitive skills for learning to decrease the estimated likelihood of negative events and/or the perceived intensity of the negative event should enhance extinction of CRs during exposure therapy. Davey (2006) refers to these as cognitive revaluation strategies, or strategies for changing the outcome expectancy of an aversive event and for devaluing its aversiveness.

In the case of substance use disorders, research similarly indicates that expectancy biases may enhance appetitive conditioning. For example, an inflated expectancy for drugs to have positive effects, such as improving mood state, has been shown to be related to the development of substance related problems (e.g., Smith, Goldman, Greenbaum, & Christiansen, 1995). These positive expectancies may enhance appetitive conditioning and again be an appropriate target during cue exposure.

Learning Theory: Instrumental Conditioning

Whereas classical conditioning principles are based on the association between a neutral stimulus and an innately evocative stimulus, instrumental conditioning principles are based on the consequences of a response and their effect on the future occurrence of that response. The basic law of learning that was originally formulated by Thorndike (1932) stated that responses followed by a "satisfier" strengthen the association between the response and the situation in which it occurred. Thus, the response would be more likely to occur in that situation in the future. As an example, if a child's oppositional behavior is followed by parental attention, then the oppositional behavior will be more likely to occur in the presence of the parent in the future. If a response is followed by an "annoyer," then the association is weakened, so that the response would be less likely to occur in that situation in the future. As an example, if a child's oppositional behavior is ignored, it would be less likely to occur in the future. Skinner (1938) developed and refined Thorndike's theory; he rejected Thorndike's notion of "satisfaction" and introduced his operant theory of behavior, in which the term *operants* describes classes of behavior that operate on the environment to produce certain consequences.

The consequences of behavioral responses are categorized according to their effects. There are reinforcers, which cause a behavior to occur with greater frequency, and punishers, which cause a behavior to occur with less frequency. Reinforcers and punishers are either positive, meaning they are delivered followed a response, or negative, meaning they are withdrawn following a response. Thus, an event presented immediately following a behavior that causes the behavior to increase in frequency is called a *positive reinforcer*. For example, sensory stimulation effects are believed to be a positive reinforcer for many repetitive habits such as hair pulling; in other words, hair pulling is more likely to happen in the future because it is followed by sensory stimulation. An event that increases a behavior by virtue of its withdrawal is called a negative reinforcer. For example, reduction of distress may be a *negative reinforcer* of compulsive behaviors in persons with obsessive compulsive disorder; in other words, they are more likely to engage in compulsive behaviors in the future because the compulsive behavior is followed by feeling less distressed.

Any event presented immediately following the behavior that causes the behavior to decrease in frequency is called a *positive punisher*. These include physical punishers, such as unpleasant odors, which have been used as punishers of inappropriate sexual urges, and verbal punishers, such as a stern "no" from a parent in response to a child's oppositional behavior. *Negative punishment* occurs when a behavior is followed by the removal of something positive, so that the behavior is less likely to occur again. An example is the removal from a situation in which one would otherwise be able to earn reinforcers, as is the case when children are assigned to "time out" for oppositional behavior. Another example of a negative punisher is the deduction from a person's collection of reinforcers, also termed *response cost*, as is sometimes used in behavioral diet and exercise programs; for example, if more than a maximum number of calories is consumed, or if less than a minimum amount of exercise is completed, the client agrees to give her own money to a nonpreferred charity. Extinction is the lack of any consequence following a behavior; inconsequential behavior, without any favorable or unfavorable consequences, will lessen in frequency.

The effectiveness of reinforcers and punishers is influenced by factors such as satiation, or the degree to which the individual's appetite for the consequence has been already satisfied. For example, food is sometimes used as a reinforcer for shaping verbal skills in children with autism; the effectiveness of the food reinforcer will be enhanced if the training is conducted when the child is hungry. Another factor is immediacy, with more immediate consequences having greater impact than more distal consequences. Thus, a parent's verbal reprimand of a child's misbehavior will be more effective as a positive punisher if delivered immediately after the misbehavior compared to at the end of the day. Contingency is another factor, meaning that the reliability with which the consequence follows the behavior increases its impact. For example, token reinforcers (or secondary reinforcers, which can be later exchanged for a primary reinforcer, such as food) that are delivered only some of the intervals of time in which drug abusers successfully abstain from drug use will be less effective than if they were delivered every interval of time in which abstention occurred. Finally, size of the consequence is important, with larger consequences having greater impact than smaller ones.

A good example of the application of operant principles to the understanding of psychopathology is in the area of depression. Specifically, Lewinsohn (1974) and colleagues attributed depressed mood to a low rate of response contingent positive reinforcement. Insufficient reinforcement in major life domains is presumed to lead to dysphoria and a reduction in behavior (i.e., motor retardation). Three main sources of low rates of positive reinforcement were recognized. First, the environment may produce a loss of reinforcement or be inadequate in providing sufficient reinforcement. For example, loss of a job would produce a loss of reinforcement, and chronic lack of employment would represent continuing lack of reinforcement. Second, the individual may lack the skills needed to obtain reinforcement that is potentially available. This would be the case for the person who lacks social skills and therefore misses out on the positive reinforcement from social relationships. Third, reinforcers may be available, but the individual is unable to enjoy or receive satisfaction from them, as would occur for an individual who is highly anxious in social situations to the point that the anxiety interferes with the natural positive reinforcement from social relationships. In terms of depression, it is further recognized that the negative mood may elicit positive reinforcement from others in the form of concern, resulting in the individual receiving reinforcement for behaving in a depressed manner. Such reinforcement may contribute to the maintenance of depressed behavior. However, over longer periods of time, the initial concern that is expressed by others often shifts to aversion (because continued depressed behavior eventually becomes unpleasant), resulting in eventual alienation and the withdrawal of positive reinforcement from others. Hence, the depressed individual lacks positive reinforcement for nondepressed behaviors, is initially reinforced for depressed behaviors, and then eventually loses reinforcement for any kind of behavior.

Another application of operant principles is in disorders related to substance use. Drug use is believed to be maintained by the positively reinforcing effects of the physiological effects of the drugs, as well as social reinforcement, such as peer approval, that is given to a drug-abusing lifestyle. In addition, the escape that drugs provide from life stressors, negative mood states, or even the withdrawal effects from the drugs themselves negatively reinforce drug-taking behavior.

Principles of Treatment

In operant methodologies to treatment, a functional analysis is conducted to evaluate the factors that may be contributing to excesses of maladaptive behavior and/or deficits of adaptive behaviors, and interventions are designed to alter the antecedents to behaviors, and to use reinforcers to enhance adaptive behaviors and punishers or extinction to decrease maladaptive behaviors. More specifically, the functional analysis establishes the causal relations between antecedents to a behavior, the behavior, and the consequences of a behavior. For example, as described by Farmer and Chapman (2008), bulimia might involve antecedent events of conflict with significant others and proximity to a food market that precede the behavior of overeating. This behavior is positively reinforced by the immediate gratification of eating. The subsequent discomfort from overeating then becomes an antecedent to the next behavior of purging, which in turn is followed by negative reinforcement of reduction in discomfort. The positive reinforcement of immediate gratification of eating and the negative reinforcement of reduction of discomfort through purging increase the likelihood of the binging and purging cycle in the future. Understanding the "behavioral contingencies" of any given problem behavior is essential to effective treatment planning.

A behavior is said to be under stimulus control when it occurs in the presence of a particular stimulus and not in its absence. Following the previous example, the bulimic behavior may occur only in relation to conflict with a significant other. In this case, conflict with others becomes a discriminative stimulus for the behavior of overeating. Oftentimes, the discriminative stimuli are moderated by other ongoing contextual variables, such as time of day and mood state, so that the relationships become relatively complex. In the aggregate, the discriminative stimuli and associated conditions function to signal the likelihood of reinforcing or punishing consequences of the behavior. Another type of antecedent is termed *establishing operations*, or events or biological conditions that alter the reinforcing or punishing consequences. Continuing with the example of bulimia, having recently dieted may serve as an establishing operation that magnifies the likelihood of immediate gratification from overeating (i.e., the principle of satiation) in the presence of the cue of conflict with others. The role of discriminative stimuli and establishing operations is included in the behavioral contingency formulation, which is then used to develop a treatment plan.

Behavioral contingency management involves changing the antecedents of the target behavior, such as removing or avoiding the antecedents that typically elicit problem behaviors. This strategy is typically included in treatments for disorders related to substance use in which abusers are asked to avoid drug-associated people, places, and stimuli. Also, it may be used when self-injurious behaviors are under the control of certain antecedent stimuli. When the antecedent stimulus cannot be avoided completely, another strategy is to modify it. For example, recovered alcohol abusers may not be able to fully avoid peers with whom alcohol was previously consumed; in this case, the peers (the antecedents) may be asked to refrain from encouraging the recovered person from drinking. Another strategy involving antecedents is to use stimulus cues to encourage adaptive behaviors, such as "coping cards" to remind clients to engage in particular behaviors. In discrimination training, reinforcers for behaviors are given in certain situations but not in other situations, so that individuals learn in which situations particular behaviors are appropriate (if reinforced) or not (if not reinforced). As an example, in the context of anxiety disorders, approach behavior toward nondangerous situations (e.g., walking alone during the day in a safe park) would be reinforced whereas approach to truly dangerous situations (e.g., walking alone at night in a violent crime district) would not. Discrimination training can be applied to emotional states as well, such as learning to accurately discriminate between tension and relaxation, or anger and anxiety. Another strategy is to arrange establishing operations that change the value of reinforcers, as occurs when methadone decreases the reinforcement value of heroin use (by blocking the high from heroin) or when regulation of eating to four to six times a day decreases the reinforcement value of binging. Similarly, satiation therapy involves overdelivery of reinforcers that in turn is presumed to decrease their value. For example, smoking cessation programs sometimes include a period of oversmoking to decrease the reinforcement value of the nicotine.

Another set of principles for behavioral contingency management involves altering the consequences of behavior. Consequences are applied to either increase the likelihood of a desired behavior occurring again in the future (reinforcers) or decrease the likelihood of undesirable behaviors in the future (punishers), keeping in mind the factors already described as being influential, such as immediacy, size, and contingency of the consequence. An example of applying a positive reinforcer would be to praise a child who bravely approaches an anxiety-provoking situation. Interventions designed to decrease a target behavior may include extinction, or removing reinforcers that previously maintained the behavior. An example would be removal of parental attention from a child's display of oppositional behavior. Alternatively, punishers may be administered, such as negative punishers in the form of response cost (e.g., time out for oppositional behavior in children) or positive punishers as in covert sensitization procedures (Cautela, 1967). In the latter, an undesired behavior is paired in imagination with aversive states, such as pairing alcohol consumption with nausea and vomiting. Covert sensitization also includes negative reinforcement in the form of relief from the aversive state as the undesired behavior is replaced by a desired behavior.

For contingency management to work, reinforcers for adaptive behaviors must exceed the reinforcers for maladaptive behaviors. Thus, if reinforcement for consuming alcohol is more potent and immediate than it is for engaging in behaviors that do not involve alcohol, such as exercising or other forms of social recreation, then the individual will devote more time and energy to consuming alcohol. Obviously, the challenge for treatment is to make the reinforcements for adaptive behavior more influential than the reinforcements for maladaptive behavior.

As outlined by Farmer and Chapman (2008), "the primary assumption underlying contingency management interventions is that the target behavior in question is under the influence of direct-acting environmental antecedents or consequences" (p 108). Contingency management procedures are not as effective for rule-governed behavior, or behavior that is not controlled by the environmental antecedents or consequences but instead is controlled by rules. Farmer and Chapman give the example of a person with anorexia who restricts intake of food based on a rule that "by not eating, I will lose weight and be more attractive to others." This rule implies that thinness is associated with a variety of social reinforcers. However, the rule may be at odds with actual social reinforcement patterns, since others may not respond to thinness as being more attractive. Hence, the behavior of food restriction becomes more of a rule-governed behavior. In this case, behavioral contingency interventions are not useful, and direct challenges to rule governing would be more appropriate.

Another assumption of behavioral contingency programs is that the individual has the target behavior in his/her repertoire. If, for example, the target behavior is to refuse peer pressure to use drugs, and the individual is deficit in skills of assertive communication, then reliance on changes to the reinforcers and punishers of the desired behavior will have little effect. Instead, other principles would be used to develop new behaviors of assertiveness, such as response shaping and building skills. Response shaping is designed to develop behavioral skills through successive approximation to an end goal, with reinforcement for each approximation along the way. For example, in biofeedback treatment for headaches, individuals learn to lower their muscle tension. Each time their muscle tension is successfully lowered by a specified degree, an audio and/or visual signal is displayed, which reinforces the successful reduction in muscle tension. Over time, the amount by which the muscle tension has to reduce in order to be reinforced progressively increases (i.e., successive approximation). Another example of shaping is the training of communication skills in the context of severe developmental disorders; positive reinforcers are provided first for any vocalization, followed by reinforcement for vocalization of a word, then a chain of words, and so on until reinforcement applies to a full sentence. In other words, shaping involves breaking down a behavior into its components. Reinforcement is given as the client performs the initial behavior, and once that behavior is established, then reinforcement is withheld until the client performs the next behavior in the sequence.

When a certain behavior can be performed in one situation but not another, then skills training is less relevant, and instead attention may be given to response generalization. An example might be the ability to say "no" to unreasonable requests from family members but not from friends. In this case, instruction and role playing may be used to help clients perform the behavior in different contexts.

Role of Cognitive Variables in Instrumental Conditioning

In instrumental theorizing, thinking can be viewed as a form of behavior and, as such, can serve several functions. Thoughts may serve as a discriminative stimulus for behaviors, such as when thoughts about the dangers of driving lead to avoidance of driving. Thoughts may serve as establishing operations that alter the perceived consequences of behavior, such as when the thought that "if I drink alcohol, I will feel better" leads to increased drinking . Thoughts may also function as reinforcing or punishing consequences, such as positive thoughts about one's success or negative thoughts about one's failure in a given situation. Or, thoughts may function as rules that govern behavior. In all of these cases, thoughts are viewed in terms of their function and not their content.

Furthermore, as with classical conditioning, early mechanistic models of operant theorizing have been replaced by expectancy models, in which conditioning is presumed to result in the formation of representations of the relationship between a response and an outcome. That is, instrumental (operant) learning situations produce expectancies that certain behaviors will produce particular outcomes (see Kirsch et al., 2004, for a review). As with classical conditioning, there is some evidence that explicit expectancies may even mediate operant conditioning. For example, simply informing participants about response-reinforcement contingencies can produce instrumental learning, just as can information that the contingency is no longer present produce extinction. In addition, devaluing the value of the reinforcer reduces the operant responding because motivation for the outcome has presumably declined. On the other hand, there appear to be some occasions when instrumental conditioning proceeds without explicit cognitive mediation. For example, in some instances devaluation of the reinforcer has no effect (see Kirsch et al., 2004). Hence, both mechanistic and explicit cognitive processes may underlie instrumental conditioning.

Nonetheless, recognition of the role of expectancies in instrumental conditioning allows an integration between instrumental learning theory and cognitive theory. The expectancy for positive reinforcement and the perceived value of such reinforcement—and similarly the expectancy for punishment and its perceived value—likely represent individual difference variables that contribute to the potency of reinforcement and punishment. For example, depressed mood and lowered motivation to respond in general may be in part due to lowered expectancy of reinforcement. Similarly, a tendency to devalue received reinforcement (e.g, disregarding a compliment as "fake") may contribute to the behavioral deficits of depression. Conversely, antisocial behavior may be in part due to lowered expectancy of punishment and/or lowered value of received punishment (e.g., disregard for the threat of pain from a physical confrontation). Consequently, cognitive methods can be incorporated into instrumental behavioral procedures to enhance the value of the consequences being used to modify behavior. For example, cognitive therapy that enhances the expectancy and/or value of positive reinforcement can be combined with behavioral exercises designed to increase positive reinforcement, whether it be exercise, social interaction, or work performance.

Social Learning Theory: Self-Efficacy Theory

Social learning theory was first proposed by Rotter (1954) but made more popular by Bandura (1969) whose research on observational learning—learning behaviors through the observation of others' modeling such behaviors—pointed to the role of cognitive variables as powerful influences of behavior. Bandura proposed that motivation, a primary determinant of the activation and persistence of behavior, is influenced by cognitive processes of representing future consequences in thought, goal setting, and self-evaluation. As such, Bandura's work contributed to the paradigmatic shift from purely mechanistic models of learning to more cognitive models of learning, in line with Tolman (1948) and Rescorla (1968).

A specific cognitive mediator identified by Bandura is self-efficacy, or "the conviction that one can successfully execute the behavior required to produce an outcome" (Bandura, 1977, p. 193). Self-efficacy is distinct from the more general term of self-confidence, because self-efficacy is a situationally specific belief in being able to carry out a specific act, such as the ability to approach a feared object under specified conditions. Self-efficacy also is theoretically distinct from outcome expectancies, which refer to the perceived likelihood and valence of events. Outcome expectancies are the types of expectancies presumed to operate within classical and instrumental conditioning. Thus, Bandura's concept of self-efficacy was a new addition to expectancy–learning theory.

In a reciprocal determinism model, self-efficacy expectations are claimed to influence choice of behaviors and determine the degree of effort expended and persistence in the face of obstacles or aversive experiences. In other words, self-efficacy is believed to influence coping in difficult situations. Self-efficacy also is purported to contribute to thoughts and emotional reactions. For example, poor self-efficacy is presumed to contribute to excessive dwelling on personal deficiencies that in turn creates stress and impairs performance by reducing concentration on the task at hand.

Skills and incentives are additional essential determinants of action that reciprocally influence self-efficacy. Positive incentives, for example, foster performance accomplishments that raise self-efficacy, as do knowledge and skills. Also, verbal persuasion, vicarious experience, and physiological arousal are assumed to influence self-efficacy. However, the strongest influence on self-efficacy was believed to derive from performance accomplishment, because it provides the most evidence for personal achievement and skills. Even so, within a reciprocal determinism model, cognitive factors can mitigate the effects of performance success, such as when success is attributed to external factors versus oneself.

Principles of Treatment

Bandura (1977) proposed that therapeutic gains are attributable to raising and strengthening percepts of self-efficacy. Since performance accomplishment per se was considered to be the most powerful source for raising self-efficacy, his model of therapeutic change has been applied mostly to behavioral treatments (e.g., Bandura, 1988), rather than cognitive therapy. In fact, self-efficacy theory guided a specific approach to exposure therapy for anxiety disorders called *mastery exposure therapy* (Williams & Zane, 1989).

Cognitive Appraisal Theory

The primary assumption of cognitive therapy is that distorted and dysfunctional thinking is the primary determinant of mood and behavior. Thus, the impact of environmental events is presumed to be mediated by the interpretations given to them. Differing emphasis is given to the role of the environment: Constructivists, for example, view a cognitively constructed environment as being more influential on emotion and behavior than the physical environment. Others give the physical environment more equal footing with appraisals of the self or environment. However, all cognitive theorists assume that distorted thinking is common to all psychological disorders. Each disorder or each individual is characterized by a set of specific distortions and underlying core beliefs. Thus, a *content* approach to cognition is taken to emphasize the stated beliefs and appraisals. Two main cognitive theories are reviewed in the following section: rational emotive–behavior therapy (Ellis) and cognitive therapy (Beck).

Ellis and Rational–Emotive Behavior Therapy.

Ellis, like Beck, was originally trained in psychoanalysis but became dissatisfied with the inefficiency of that approach. His own approach was based on the ancient Stoic philosophy of Epictetus and the like who stated that facts do not upset people, but rather people upset themselves with the view that they take of those facts. Ellis (1962) believed that emotional reactions are mediated by "internal sentences," or thoughts, and that maladaptive responses reflect the internal sentences becoming indiscriminate and resulting in situations being labeled irrationally. Thus, even though an emotional reaction may be appropriate to the label that is attached to a situation, the label itself may be inaccurate. For example, a situation may be labeled as dangerous, in which case a fear response is appropriate, and yet the situation is not truly dangerous and therefore the label is inappropriate. Ellis (1962) suggested that such labeling of situations derives from a set of ideas that are irrational, meaning that they are not likely to be supported or confirmed by the environment, and that they lead to inappropriate negative emotions in the face of difficulty. Irrational ideas in turn are presumed to derive from various socialization experiences. Rational beliefs, or beliefs that promote survival and happiness and are likely to find empirical support in the environment, lead to appropriate emotional and behavioral responses to losses and difficulties.

Ellis proposed an ABC model of psychological functioning and disturbance, in which undesirable activating events are experienced (A), about which there are rational and irrational beliefs (B); rational beliefs create appropriate emotional and behavioral consequences (C) whereas irrational beliefs create inappropriate and dysfunctional consequences (C). This model is shown in Figure 3.1.

Thus, activating events (A) do not directly cause emotional and behavioral consequences (C); instead, beliefs (B) about those events are the most critical causes of the consequences. In his own words, Ellis (2003) characterized irrational beliefs as being rigid and extreme, inconsistent with social reality, illogical or nonsensical, demanding and "musturbatory" (i.e., must statements), "awfulizing and terribilizing" (i.e., catastrophizing), and depreciative of human worth. They represent implicit assumptions that determine how individuals judge themselves and others, and they become

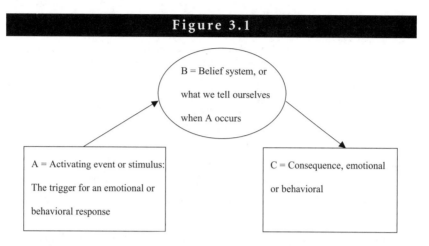

Figure 3.1

automatic and seemingly involuntary as a result of overlearning through repeated use. The most common 12 irrational beliefs are shown in Table 3.1.

Beck and Cognitive Therapy.

Beck (1976) similarly posited that much of emotional distress is due to problematic and inflexible ways of thinking. Consequently, even if individuals elicited positive reinforcement from their environment, cognitive biases would prevent them from benefiting emotionally from the reinforcement.[2] Also, negative beliefs are hypothesized to interfere with behaviors that would otherwise elicit positive reinforcement and/or produce behaviors that lead to negative consequences. This is most evident in depression, where, for example, negative thoughts about the self may lead to negative self-talk in interactions with others. Such negative self-talk may be experienced as aversive by others, who therefore avoid the speaker in the future. The resultant social isolation then contributes to further depression, but importantly, the isolation is generated in the first place by negative thinking. Negative beliefs are hypothesized to derive from genetic predispositions, modeling of cognitive style by primary care

---

[2] Noteworthy is the overlap between cognitive theory and expectancy-based models of instrumental learning.

Table 3.1

Ellis's Irrational Beliefs

1. The idea that it is a dire necessity for adults to be loved by significant others for almost everything they do—instead of concentrating on their own self-respect, on winning approval for practical purposes, and on loving rather than on being loved.

2. The idea that certain acts are awful or wicked and that people who perform such acts should be severely damned—instead of the idea that certain acts are self-defeating or antisocial and that people who perform such acts are behaving stupidly, ignorantly, or neurotically and would be better helped to change. People's poor behavior does not make them rotten individuals.

3. The idea that it is horrible when things are not the way we like them to be—instead of the idea that it is too bad, that we would better try to change or control bad conditions so that they become more satisfactory, and, if that is not possible, we had better temporarily accept and gracefully lump their existence.

4. The idea that human misery is invariably externally caused and is forced on us by outside people and events—instead of the idea that neurosis is largely caused by the view that we take of unfortunate conditions.

5. The idea that if something is or may be dangerous or fearsome, we should be terribly upset and endlessly obsess about it—instead of the idea that one would better frankly face it and render it nondangerous and, when that is not possible, accept the inevitable.

6. The idea that it is easier to avoid than to face life difficulties and self-responsibilities—instead of the idea that the so-called easy way is usually much harder in the long run.

7. The idea that we absolutely need something other or stronger or greater than ourselves on which to rely—instead of the idea that it is better to take the risks of thinking and acting less dependently.

8. The idea that we should be thoroughly competent, intelligent, and achieving in all possible respects—instead of the idea that we would better do rather than always need to do well and accept ourselves as imperfect creatures, who have general human limitations and specific fallibilities.

9. The idea that because something once strongly affected our lives, it should indefinitely affect it—instead of the idea that we can learn from our past experiences but not be overly attached to or prejudiced by them.

10. The idea that we must have certain and perfect control over things—instead of the idea that the world is full of probability and chance and that we can still enjoy life despite this.

Table 3.1 (*Continued*)

11. The idea that human happiness can be achieved by inertia and inaction—instead of the idea that we tend to be happiest when we are vitally absorbed in creative pursuits or when we are devoting ourselves to people or projects outside ourselves.

12. The idea that we have virtually no control over our emotions and that we cannot help feeling disturbed about things—instead of the idea that we have real control over our destructive emotions if we choose to work at changing the musturbatory hypotheses we often employ to create them.

givers, and adverse life events. Also, negative thoughts are believed to remain dormant until activated by negative mood states or stressful life events, particularly those that match the content of the negative beliefs.

Beck's approach has evolved considerably over time. Indeed, one of the criticisms has been its changing nature, in that terms are replaced by new terms or the same terms are used to reflect different concepts. In its more recent forms, the approach uses a computer-based model of information processing. As Beck himself noted,

> Simply stated, the cognitive model of psychopathology stipulates that the processing of external events or internal stimuli is biased and therefore systematically distorts the individual's construction of his or her experiences, leading to a variety of cognitive errors (e.g., overgeneralization, selective abstraction, and personalization). Underlying these distorted interpretations are dysfunctional beliefs incorporated into relatively enduring cognitive structures or schemas. When these schemas are activated by external events, drugs, or endocrine factors, they tend to bias the information processing and produce the typical cognitive content of a specific disorder. (2005, p. 953)

Clark, Beck, and Alford (1999) outlined 11 basic assumptions of Beck's cognitive information processing model:

1. The capacity to form cognitive representations of the self and the environment is central to human adaptation and survival. Other terms used interchangeably with cognitive representations are *meaning structures and schemas* (the latter term is used herein). A schema is conceptualized as an

internal model of the self and the world that is used to perceive, code, and recall information. Schemas are adaptive to the degree that they facilitate the processing of the extensive amount of information we encounter in daily life. However, as social and cognitive psychologists have noted for some time, the need for efficiency results in natural biases toward encoding and retrieving information that is consistent with a schema at the cost of information that is inconsistent. Such biases are believed to contribute to the persistence of schemas over time.

2. Human information processing is presumed to occur at different levels of consciousness extending from the preconscious, unintentional automatic level to the highly effortful, elaborative conscious level. In cognitive therapy, conscious appraisals are viewed as a valid data point.

3. A basic function of information processing is the personal construction of reality, as represented in schemas, but, in contrast to "constructivism," which denies an objective reality, Beck's cognitive theory and therapy subscribes to a dual existence involving an objective reality and a personal, subjective phenomenological reality.

4. Information processing serves as a guiding principle for the emotional, behavioral, and physiological components of human experience. Also, each affective state and psychological disorder has its own specific cognitive profile (i.e., cognitive content specificity), and the cognitive content determines the type of emotional experience or psychological disturbance that is experienced. Thus, depression and sadness involve appraisals of loss or failure, happiness involves thoughts of personal gain, anxiety and fear involve evaluations of threats or danger, and anger involves appraisals of assault or transgression on one's personal domain. Furthermore, some schemas are core in that they are related to the basic sense of identity or self, whereas others are peripheral. The core schema in depression, for example, pertains to self-worth as defined by either interpersonal relations (sociotropy) or autonomous achievement (autonomy); sociotropic individuals would be more likely to become depressed in interpersonal rejection situations, whereas personal achievement stressors would be more relevant to individuals high on autonomy. Core schemas are heavily influenced not only by distortions in information processing and lack of attention to information that has disconfirmatory power, but also by behaviors that confirm the schemas. As

an example, the behavior for someone whose schema is of being unlovable may take the form of neediness, and such neediness may alienate others, which in turn confirms the schema of being unlovable.

5. Cognitive functioning consists of a continuous interaction between lower-order, stimulus driven processes and higher-order semantic processes. These are referred to as *top-down and bottom-up processes*. Information processing is seen as the *product* of higher-order, top-down processing, involving abstraction and selection, and the more basic, bottom-up processing of raw stimulus characteristics in the environment. In nonpathological states, appraisals are evenly influenced by the bottom-up situational context (i.e., empirical data) as well as by top-down, higher-order inferences. Psychopathology is caused by information relevant to the disorder becoming hyperaccessible due to dominant maladaptive schemas. These schemas result in heavy top-down influences of selection, abstraction, and elaboration of information. Hence, the dysfunctional schemas are likely to lead to dysfunctional automatic thoughts, or surface level cognitions. These thoughts are called automatic because they are often fleeting and unnoticed and are not necessarily fully conscious. Beck presumed that these appraisals led directly to situationally specific emotional and behavioral responses. Hence, a schema of being unlovable may lead an individual to appraise his partner's behavior as a sign of disinterest—when in fact the partner is preoccupied with her own concerns—leading the individual to feel sad and to become more withdrawn.

Such automatic situational appraisals are mediated by cognitive distortions in information processing. Cognitive distortions provide a bridge between automatic thoughts and schemas. That is, cognitive distortions of new or ambiguous information tend to be driven by schemas and then lead to automatic thoughts becoming accessible in consciousness. Examples of such distortions are shown in Table 3.2.

6. Schemas are at best an approximation of experience, in that all information processing is egocentric and therefore a biased representation of reality. What distinguishes cognition between disordered and nondisordered states is the degree to which the former is influenced by pre-potent dysfunctional schemas.

Table 3.2

Common Cognitive Distortions

Label	Description	Example
Dichotomous thinking	Considering only the extremes	I am a complete failure.
Overgeneralizing	A single instance is viewed as indicative of a broader class	Because I was not invited to the party, I will not be invited to other parties.
Selective abstraction	Attending to certain, usually negative, aspects of a situation at the cost of other aspects	The person at the back of the audience was not interested in what I was saying.
Mind reading	Attitudes or actions of others are assumed without evidence	She obviously thinks I don't know what I am doing.
Personalizing	Assuming that an action is directed toward or occurs because of oneself	He walked away because he doesn't want to see me.
'Should' statements	Absolute imperatives	I must be smart and witty at all times.
Catastrophizing	Anticipating extreme negative consequences without evidence	My husband hasn't called— he might be dead.
Minimizing	Downplaying the significance of positive outcomes	They only said they liked the dinner because they felt pity for me.

7. Schemas develop through repeated interactions between the environment and innate rudimentary schemas. That is, they develop by increasing elaboration and connections with other schemas, and those schemas that are activated more frequently become more elaborated and therefore more dominant in the overall organization of schemas. For example, the more often the schema of being unlovable is activated, the more likely the concept of being unlovable will dominate interpretations of ongoing situations. Furthermore, schema development is additionally influenced by genetic or biological propensities.

8. Schemas are organized in different levels. The most basic level is single schemas. Single schemas then cluster together to form nodes, or the cognitive representation of psychological disorders. Nodes then interconnect with other nodes as the cognitive representation of personality.

9. Schemas are characterized by different levels of threshold activation, which occurs through a match between stimulus features of the environment and relevant schemas. Schemas that are more frequently activated have lower thresholds for activation and thereby are hypervalent and more dominant. Dominant schemas become activated by a wide array of environmental stimuli and trivial matching stimuli; they are easily accessible, dominate information processing once activated, and resist deactivation.

10. Two general orientations are represented, the first aimed at the primary goals of the organism (or schemas involved in meeting the basic needs necessary for survival) and the second aimed at secondary constructive goals (or schemas to do with preservation, reproduction, dominance, and sociability). Most primal processing occurs at automatic or preconscious levels and tends to be rigid and inflexible, whereas processing at the secondary level is more conscious and controlled. In psychological disorders, the primary schemas have become more dominant and the constructive schemas less active.

11. Psychological disturbance usually is characterized by excessive activation of specific primal schemas that lead to narrowing of information processing and inadequate activation of other more adaptive schemas.

Cognitive Appraisal Theory and Expectancy–Learning Theory

As reviewed, classical and instrumental conditioning models incorporate cognition in the form of outcome expectancies for the likelihood and valence of the US and of consequences, respectively, with ongoing debate as to the necessity for expectancies to be explicit, conscious appraisals versus implicit, automatic representations. In contrast, cognitive appraisal theory is essentially about the content of cognitions at the level of explicit, conscious appraisals.[3]

These theories can be intertwined in a number of ways, including the contribution of instrumental and classical conditioning to the development of conscious appraisals. For example, persons who have been traumatized (i.e., classical aversive conditioning) are likely to develop beliefs about the world as being a dangerous place; and persons who are not positively

---

[3] Beck's model recognizes the role of subconscious cognitive processes, but the immediate target of cognitive therapy is conscious cognitive appraisals.

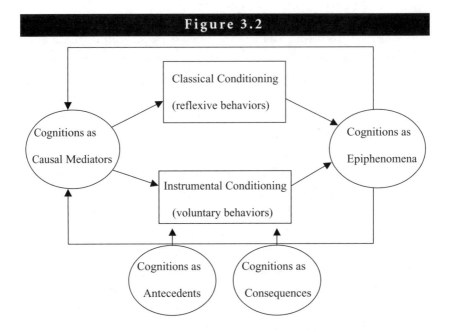

Figure 3.2

reinforced for their efforts may develop negative beliefs about themselves or the world. In this way, cognitions can be considered the epiphenomena of conditioning. Once acquired, these cognitions may then feed back to influence subsequent learning experiences by influencing expectancies for US and/or for consequences. Thus, a belief that the world is a dangerous place may become a causal mediator in future learning experiences, because the belief increases the expectancy of aversive events. For example, following criticism from a peer, expectancies for more and greater criticism are likely to increase the chances of becoming conditionally fearful as a result of negative social interactions in the future. Similarly, a negative belief about oneself, which developed out of lack of positive reinforcement, may become a causal mediator by contributing to the devaluation of future reinforcers, thereby leading to further loss of positive reinforcement. These interrelations are depicted in Figure 3.2. Note that this figure does not include two important issues: the myriad of other sociocultural and biological factors, aside from conditioning, that contribute to beliefs and the aspects of classical and instrumental conditioning that may occur without conscious cognitive mediation (see Kirsch et al., 2004).

Principles of Treatment

The primary assumption of cognitive therapy, whether in accordance with Ellis or Beck, is that dysfunctional thinking can be changed and, in turn, lead to symptomatic relief and improvement in functioning. Ellis noted that "Being constructivists (both innately and by social learning), and having language to help them, they are also able to think about their thinking, and even think about thinking about their thinking. Therefore, they can therapeutically choose to change their IBs [irrational beliefs] to more rational (self-helping) beliefs" (2003, p. 80).

A key concept is the development of alternative cognitive content that is more realistic and evidence-based and less governed by core irrational beliefs or schemas. Hence, the focus is on changing the *content* of beliefs, automatic thoughts, and assumptions. As Clark and colleagues (1999) note:

> The degree of symptomatic improvement brought about by these interventions will depend on the extent of change produced in the information processing system. Moreover, recovery will be more enduring and relapse reduced if the underlying maladaptive meaning-structures, and not just negative thinking, are targeted for change during treatment. (p. 70)

Conscious reasoning is used to change in the content of beliefs. According to Beck and Clark (1997), "one of the most effective ways of deactivating the primal threat mode is to counter it with more elaborative, strategic processing of information resulting from the activation of the constructive, reflective modes of thinking" (p. 55). Cognitive therapy represents such elaborative, strategic processing. Thus, cognitive therapy functions at the conscious level to effect changes in the preconscious level.

However, the mechanism by which primal automatic thoughts are changed by more elaborative strategic thoughts is not well understood. Several models of change in cognition exist (Garratt, Ingram, Rand, & Sawalani, 2007). The accommodation model assumes that the content of underlying schemas is changed in profound ways. Another model, known as the activation-deactivation model, suggests that the schemas remain intact but become deactivated over the course of treatment. In a third model, schemas may remain unchanged, but new schemas develop as a result of therapy and these schemas incorporate skills for dealing with stressful situations (Garratt et al., 2007). However, the data on mechanisms are sparse (as described in more detail in a following section) and the precise mechanisms through which beliefs change remain unclear.

Another concept key to cognitive therapy is an empiricist approach. This involves incorporating more bottom-up processes rather than being predominantly driven by inferences or top-down processes that are guided by maladaptive schemas or illogical thinking. An empiricist approach also involves developing an awareness of one's own thinking and learning to distance, or view one's thoughts more objectively and to draw a distinction between "I believe" (an option that is open to disconfirmation) and "I know" (an irrefutable fact). Skills are taught not only for how to identify distortions in thinking but also how to categorize and distance from negative thoughts and how to develop more evidence-based and constructive thinking. Behavioral experimentation is used to gather evidence for the formation of more constructive thinking. These skills are then employed whenever negative emotions or dysfunctional behaviors are expressed. Hence, the skills provide a coping tool that is intended to remain in place and even strengthen after formal treatment is over. Cognitive therapy does not aim to teach accuracy in appraisals. Rather "the more relevant question is whether the person is able to conceptualize the situation in a manner that will facilitate mastery or coping" (Clark, Beck, & Alford, 1999, p. 64). Learning to have flexibility in thinking and the ability to take multiple perspectives rather than a single narrow interpretation is a way of facilitating mastery and coping.

In sum, the fundamental process of cognitive therapy is to extract information from the environment that activates different ways of thinking. In Beck's model in particular, this information is intended to compete with dysfunctional schemas or generate compensatory schemas that deactivate dysfunctional hypervalent schemas. The attainment of information occurs in a number of ways, including logical discussion of the evidence, disputation, and behavioral experimentation to gather evidence.

Cognitive–Behavioral Theory

Cognitive–behavioral theories of psychopathology and psychotherapy draw on learning theory as well as cognitive theory principles described thus far: CRs for innately aversive or appetitive events and the role of expectancies in the generation of those responses; instrumental learning from the consequences of responding and the role of expectancies on that learning; reciprocal determinism among cognitions, behaviors, and the environment from social learning theory; and the content of cognitive appraisals. Conceptually, these are intertwined, with behavioral experience molding cognitions and cognitions molding behavioral experience in a continuous, reciprocating fashion. As previously described, cognition can be regarded as a product and as a mediator of instrumental and classical learning, and learning can be regarded as a contributor to conscious cognition. Consequently, treatment is guided by the influence of learning experiences on cognition and the influence of cognition on learning experiences.

In the cognitive–behavioral model of posttraumatic stress disorder, for example, the initial traumatic event is assumed to establish classically conditioned fear reactions to reminders of the trauma. In addition, the effects of the trauma, including the extent of the conditional responding, are assumed to be enhanced by catastrophic appraisals about the meaning of the trauma with regard to oneself (e.g., "I am weak") and the world ("The world is full of danger"). Together, these processes lead to avoidance behavior, which in turn is reinforced by the reduction in distress it produces, and which also perpetuates conditional fear (because avoidance interrupts extinction) and catastrophic appraisals.

Similarly, in the cognitive–behavioral model of substance use disorders, antecedents to drug use behavior are assumed to be established through repeated pairings with positive or negative reinforcement or through the anticipation of reinforcement. Cognitions, such as expectancies about the reinforcing value of the drug effects, and emotions, such as distress or anger, are presumed to mediate the antecedents and subsequent drug use behavior. Furthermore, drug use behavior is presumed to be maintained by its consequences, be it decreased craving or decreased withdrawal symptoms, decreases in negative affect or increases in positive affect, or decreased focus on other problems and concerns. Also, negative beliefs about the self or the world may contribute to the negative affect from which the drug serves as an escape.

In the cognitive–behavioral model of depression, emphasis is given to the lack of positive reinforcement derived from the environment, some of which may be attributed to independent factors over which the individual has no control and others that are likely to derive from the individual's own actions. An example of the latter is interpersonal conflict and isolation that occurs in part as a result of the individual's own depressive interpersonal style. The latter behaviors are themselves likely to be influenced by negative appraisals of oneself or the world, and their consequences serve to only reinforce the negative appraisals in a reciprocating style. Negative appraisals themselves also are likely to devalue the reinforcers that are received from the environment.

In one more example, the cognitive–behavioral model of chronic pain recognizes the role of conditional pain behaviors to reminders of pain (e.g., a doctor's office), the role of reinforcement in the maintenance of pain behavior (e.g., attention from significant others, escape from unpleasant tasks or duties), and the effects of cognitive appraisals on the perceived intensity and unmanageability of pain, which in turn are likely to magnify CRs and the reinforcement of pain behavior.

Clinicians vary in the emphasis given to cognitive versus behavioral principles. This variation influences subtleties in the ways in which cognitive and behavioral intervention strategies are implemented. For example, a more behaviorally oriented clinician will view exposure therapy to feared situations as a primary vehicle for extinction of CRs. A social learning theory orientation views exposure therapy as a performance accomplishment that raises self-efficacy. A more cognitively oriented clinician will view exposure therapy as a vehicle for obtaining information that disconfirms misappraisals.

4

The Therapy Process

Cognitive–behavioral therapy (CBT) typically involves a series of components. A functional analysis usually initiates the treatment, in order to establish not just the topography of the problem behaviors, emotions, and cognitions but also their functional relationships with each other and to identify the factors that may cause, contribute to, or exacerbate a particular problem. This includes a consideration of the antecedents and consequences of behavior; the stimuli that are eliciting cognitive, emotional, and behavioral conditional responses (CRs); and identification of which cognitions are contributing to which emotions and behaviors. The effect of environmental and cultural context on these relationships is evaluated as well. Self-monitoring helps to refine the functional analysis and generate a personal scientist perspective (or, being an objective observer of one's own reactions) of the interplay of thoughts, emotions, and behaviors in given contexts. The functional analysis then guides the treatment approach. Behavioral strategies target ways of increasing desirable behaviors and decreasing undesirable behaviors through control of antecedents, changing patterns of reinforcers, building skills, or exposure-based procedures for weakening learned associations. Cognitive strategies include identifying and challenging dysfunctional cognitions through logical empiricism, disputation, or behavioral experimentation. Each strategy is described in more detail in this chapter.

ROLE OF THERAPIST–CLIENT RELATIONSHIP

Unlike many other therapies, the client–therapist relationship is not viewed as a primary vehicle of therapy in CBT. Rather, the behavioral experiences that are arranged for the client and the cognitive and behavioral coping skills that are taught are presumed to serve as the primary agents of change. However, that does not mean that the therapist–client relationship is irrelevant, as it is generally recognized that qualities of the therapist–client relationship form an important base from which the various CBT strategies are implemented. Thus, "the truly skillful behavior therapist is one who can both conceptualize problems behaviorally and make the necessary translations so that he interacts in a warm and empathic manner with his client" (Goldfried & Davison, 1994, p. 56). Indeed, the evidence indicates that CBT is more effective when delivered within a warm and empathic environment, particularly in the first few treatment sessions (e.g., Keijsers, Schaap, Hoogduin, & Lammers, 1995).

A strong feature of the therapist–client relationship in CBT is collaboration, a feature that permeates every aspect of treatment. Whereas the therapist is the expert in behavioral and cognitive science and theory and their application, the therapist is also dependent on clients' self-observation to tailor the interventions to their particular needs. Thus, the client and therapist jointly develop and refine the functional analysis and treatment plan. The therapist and client also jointly evaluate the evidence regarding the client's beliefs and assumptions and jointly design behavioral interventions for shifting patterns of reinforcement, for weakening CRs, for building skills, and for behavioral experimentation to gather information that disconfirms misappraisals. In addition, the therapist and client jointly evaluate the effectiveness of each intervention and make modifications as appropriate. Through this level of collaboration, clients acquire a set of knowledge and skills that make them more expert and eventually capable of treatment formulation, implementation, and refinement on their own.

The collaborative nature of the relationship is enhanced by emphasizing the goals, targets, and process of therapy in the first few sessions. This prepares the client for cognitive and behavioral change and active involvement in such change. Hence, in the first few sessions, treatment goals are specified, an accurate perception of the treatment process is given, and a treatment contract may be written. The contract makes it clear what is expected of the client and the therapist.

The collaborative nature of the therapist–client relationship promotes the effects of therapist reinforcement, something that is central to the therapist's role in CBT. The therapist provides reinforcement for clients' engagement in CBT and particularly for their completion of homework assignments between sessions. Client engagement in between-session assignments leads to better outcomes from CBT. Thus, treatment outcomes are enhanced by a good client–therapist relationship because it enhances the value of therapist reinforcement, which in turn increases client engagement. Similarly, CBT therapists often serve as models for clients, such as when modeling methods of approaching feared situations, or the acquisition of new skills. Again, the effectiveness of the therapist as a model probably is influenced by the nature of the therapist–client relationship.

In short, the collaborative nature of the client–therapist relationship is inherent to CBT and is considered an essential platform from which the various skills and exercises are introduced and implemented. However, there is little direct investigation of its significance. Furthermore, the extant research is contradictory. Kazdin, Marciano, and Whitley (2005) found that the therapeutic alliance, defined as the collaborative nature of the client–therapist relationship, their agreement on goals, and the personal bond between them, related positively to outcomes from CBT for oppositional, aggressive, and antisocial behavior in children. In contrast, therapeutic alliance was unrelated to the outcome from CBT for depression (Feeley, DeRubeis, & Gelfand, 1999). Moreover, rather than predicting improvements in symptoms, a positive alliance was shown to follow improvements in symptoms, at least within the course of CBT for depression (e.g., Tang & DeRubeis, 1999). Kazdin (2007) notes the methodological limitations of most existing studies of mediators of CBT, including studies of therapeutic alliance. Thus, the role of the client–therapist relationship in outcomes from CBT awaits further investigation.

ROLE OF THE THERAPIST

The CBT therapist has a number of roles to perform, some of which have been touched on in discussing the client–therapist relationship. First, the CBT therapist is a diagnostician, who takes into account the various sources of information from the client, and judging against his or her own background of knowledge, "diagnoses" the problem and optimal strategy for intervention (Kendall, 1993). That is, the CBT therapist uses his or her grounding in behavioral and cognitive science and theory to help construct a functional analysis of reinforcers, punishers, learned associations, and cognitive appraisals that together contribute to maladaptive patterns of behaving, thinking, and emoting. Through their questioning, observations, and reflections, CBT therapists model the method of being a personal scientist to the client.

The therapist also plays a role in helping clients to make guided discoveries about their own thinking. More specifically, the therapist uses a set of strategies to help clients identify and challenge their maladaptive assumptions and beliefs. These include helping clients to label their cognitive distortions, examine the evidence for and against an assumption, challenge absolute statements by using scaling, evaluate the probability of outcomes, and examine other possible explanations for events. Also, by observing common themes across different automatic thoughts, the therapist generates hypotheses regarding underlying schema. This can be further achieved by the downward arrow technique (Burns, 1980), in which the consequences of a particular thought are repeatedly drawn out to the final meaning. For example, the downward arrow technique applied to thoughts about panic attacks could involve the following:

Therapist: . . . And if you panicked, what do you envision happening?

Client: I see myself losing control.

Therapist: And if you lost control, what would that mean?

Client: I would go crazy.

Therapist: And if you went crazy, what would that mean?

Client: Then that would be the end. . . . My life would be completely gone.

Also, the therapist actively encourages clients to generate new appraisals through Socratic questioning, presenting juxtapositions between stated beliefs and empirical evidence, and reflections. Again, throughout all of these actions, the therapist is serving as a model for clients to acquire the same set of skills for their own cognitive restructuring.

Furthermore, the CBT therapist helps to design and implement behavioral strategies for changing reinforcement schedules, for increasing desired behaviors and decreasing undesired behaviors, for building new sets of associations that inhibit maladaptive ones, and for developing new skills. The CBT therapist also provides explicit and implicit reinforcement for cognitive and behavioral changes. One specific example of therapist reinforcement occurs when the therapist physically accompanies clients as they approach feared situations in the natural environment. Such therapist-directed exposure maximizes the reinforcement potential of the therapist and is particularly useful for clients who lack a social network to support their practices of approaching feared situations (Holden, O'Brien, Barlow, Stetson, & Infantino, 1983). Also, the therapist can model and guide specific behaviors in the exposure setting, as is done in "guided mastery exposure" (Williams, 1990). Williams and his colleagues have shown this type of mastery exposure to be more effective than usual exposure methods (e.g., Williams & Zane, 1989). Therapist modeling, also called participant modeling, can be conducted within the therapy office as well. For example, the therapist can be an explicit model in role plays and behavioral rehearsal for skill acquisition (e.g., assertive skills), or in behavioral practice (e.g., how to touch a previously avoided object for fears of contamination).

The therapist also may serve as an inadvertent model. "Thus, the therapist should be aware continually of his impact on the client, making every effort to model behavior, attitudes and emotions likely to enhance therapeutic progress" (Goldfried & Davison, 1994, p. 60). For example, it would not be helpful for a therapist to exhibit the same fears as the client, especially if the therapist's fears are poorly regulated. Finally, the CBT therapist reviews and troubleshoots where cognitive and behavior change is not occurring as rapidly as desired, using principles of scientific experimentation to evaluate the results of interventions and to modify them where necessary, always in collaboration with the client.

For all of these reasons, therapist experience would be expected to make a difference to the success of CBT. Only a handful of studies have investigated the topic of therapist experience or training. Huppert and colleagues (2001) demonstrated that the experience of therapists in general (versus experience with CBT more specifically) positively influenced outcome from CBT for panic disorder, seemingly because experienced therapists were more flexible in administering CBT and better able to adapt it to the individual being treated. The latter point speaks to the value of a good functional analysis to guide the application of CBT to a presenting problem. Other studies show that amount of time in training and prior experience with cognitive therapy are correlates of competency with cognitive therapy (James, Blackburn, Milne, & Reichfelt, 2001) and that additional training in CBT results in better delivery of CBT (Brosan, Reynolds, & Moore, 2007).

On the other hand, therapist experience is not a significant moderator of treatment effects in community settings (e.g., Hahlweg, Fiegenbaum, Frank, Schroeder, & von Witzleben, 2001). Also, a benchmarking study indicated that the effects for CBT for posttraumatic stress disorder conducted in community settings with a range of therapist experience were equivalent to effects obtained with highly trained CBT therapists in randomized controlled trials (Levitt, Malta, Martin, Davis, & Cloitre, 2007). Furthermore, other studies show that success can be achieved when administering CBT with minimal or no therapist contact at all.

Minimal Therapist Contact

For example, some studies have shown positive results when the therapist and client do not meet in person but rather converse by phone, at least in the treatment for agoraphobia (e.g., Swinson, Fergus, Cox, & Wickwire, 1995) and panic disorder (Cote, Gauthier, Laberge, Cormier, & Plamondon, 1994). In addition, self-directed CBT in which clients never or rarely talk with a therapist but instead are guided by workbooks and manuals are beneficial for highly motivated and educated clients with anxiety disorders (e.g., Schneider, Mataix-Cols, Marks, & Bachofen, 2005). However, self-directed treatments are less effective for more severely anxious clients or clients who have more comorbidity (e.g., Hecker, Losee, Roberson-Nay, & Maki, 2004). Also, neither phone contact nor self-directed treatments have been evaluated with severely depressed or suicidal individuals for obvious ethical reasons.

Self-directed treatments have expanded beyond workbooks and manuals to computerized and Internet versions (see Spek et al., 2007, for a meta-analysis). Stand-alone computerized versions of CBT have been found to be generally acceptable to clients and effective in treating depression and anxiety as well as specific anxiety disorders. However, computerized programs are more acceptable and more successful when clinician involvement, even minimally (e.g., telephone contact), is offered. Internet programs with minimal clinician involvement are a promising alternative when CBT clinicians are not available (e.g., rural areas), although ethical issues may be a limiting factor in some cases.

The finding that CBT can be effective in the absence of a therapist highlights the power of the strategies of CBT over the qualities of the therapist and the therapist–client relationship within CBT. The effectiveness of group formats for delivering CBT (e.g., Norton & Price, 2007) is another indicator that the particular strategies of CBT may be more important than the client–therapist relationship. Furthermore, as noted previously, range of therapist experience does not always moderate outcomes from CBT in community settings. On the other hand, experienced therapists may be more competent and effective in implementing CBT, and clients may be more likely to complete CBT if it is conducted with the aid of a therapist.

ROLE OF THE CLIENT

CBT clients are trained to become actively involved in treatment formulation and implementation, decisions about the best approaches to take, and how to modify and improve upon each intervention strategy. This active involvement is facilitated by emphasizing the general philosophy that the client is not the problem but rather the behaviors, emotions, and cognitions are the problem, for which the client and therapist are united to help solve.

For this reason, clients for whom CBT works best are motivated and value a problem-solving approach, even if they themselves have yet to learn how to implement such an approach.

More specifically, the role of the client in CBT is to participate collaboratively in the assessment and treatment process. Such engagement begins with helping clients to fully understand the treatment rationale, which in turn is tied closely to their understanding and participation in the functional analysis of their presenting problem. Hence, clients learn the skills of self-observation and of becoming a personal scientist; they become skilled in understanding the functional relations among cognitive, behavioral, and emotional responding and the relevant contextual influences.

Next, the client learns new cognitive and behavioral skills and strategies, initially with the aid of the therapist. Simultaneously, clients learn the skills of how to evaluate the results of intervention strategies, brainstorm ways of improving skill implementation, and reinforce their own efforts, with the aid of the therapist. Beyond therapist aid, however, the role of the client is to repeatedly practice the skills in personally relevant contexts outside of the therapy setting. By so doing, clients become less and less dependent on the therapist. Such practice is typically referred to as *homework*.

Homework may be one of the most distinctive features of CBT compared to other forms of psychotherapy, and one that is presumed to be critical to therapeutic change. In support, several studies, mostly regarding depression and anxiety, show a positive correlation between homework adherence and treatment outcome (see Kazantzis, Deane, & Ronan, 2002). Also, homework compliance significantly mediates outcomes (Burns & Spangler, 2000) and is related to continued improvement after CBT is completed (e.g., Edelman & Chambless, 1995).

Consequently, understanding what factors are associated with homework compliance is useful. Conoley, Padula, Payton, and Daniels (1994) found, not surprisingly, that task difficulty was negatively correlated with homework compliance. Also, Robinson (2003) suggests that clients are more likely to adhere when they participate actively in the formulation of the homework plan. Client acceptance and understanding of the treatment rationale, and expectancy for change, are other predictors of homework compliance (Westra, Dozois, & Marcus, 2007).

STRATEGIES/TECHNIQUES

The following is a relatively comprehensive, albeit not exhaustive, description of the set of cognitive and behavioral strategies that make up CBT. Broadly speaking, the strategies can be categorized as skill and reinforcement based, exposure based, and cognitively based. Skill- and reinforcement-based strategies were developed primarily or originally from an instrumental learning theory approach. Exposure-based strategies were developed primarily or originally from a classical conditioning approach, and cognitively based strategies were developed primarily or originally from cognitive theory approaches. However, the overlap across strategies is substantial at the procedural level. Furthermore, given ways in which learning theories have evolved to incorporate cognitions, and given the contribution of learning to conscious appraisals, almost all of the intervention strategies evoke mechanisms relevant to both learning theories and cognitive theories. For example, behavioral rehearsal of assertive skills is likely to involve reinforcement, extinction of CRs, as well as cognitive mechanisms. Each strategy explored in this section is accompanied by a description of potential mechanisms underlying its effectiveness (with the exception of cognitive strategies) and contraindications for its use.

Decisions about which specific strategies of CBT are likely to be most effective for a given set of symptoms are determined through a functional analysis. That is, choice of treatment strategy is based on a careful analysis of responding, including antecedents and consequences, triggering stimuli for CRs, and cognitive appraisals, as well as the surrounding environmental, cultural, and interpersonal contexts. For example, the choice between behavioral rehearsal of assertiveness versus cognitive therapy for social anxiety depends on whether the social anxiety is based on a skill deficit (in which case a behavioral rehearsal approach may be indicated, assuming it was culturally appropriate) or instead is due to the interfering effects of anxiety on social skills (possibly leading to the choice of cognitive therapy).

The complexity of the strategies described varies, ranging from very simple and focused habit reversal strategies to broader and more comprehensive approaches such as rational–emotive behavior therapy, cognitive therapy, or problem-solving therapy. Most often, single strategies are combined with other strategies to form packages of CBT. More complete examples of ways in which the strategies are combined follow the listing of each individual strategy.

Skill- and Reinforcement-Based Strategies

Self-Monitoring

In CBT, self-monitoring is a tool for evaluating the functional relations among thoughts, behaviors, and emotions, and their antecedents and consequences, as they occur (versus retrospective report). Self-monitoring is particularly valuable for recording subjective experience, such as appraisals (e.g., "My friends must think I am a fool.") and levels of subjective distress. Moreover, self-monitoring is useful for behaviors or physiological events that are difficult to record otherwise because they occur infrequently (e.g., occasional panic attacks) or under conditions that are difficult to replicate in the presence of the therapist (e.g., compulsive rituals that are dependent on the home environment; Craske & Tsao, 1999). Overall, self-monitoring is used widely across a large array of disorders and behavioral problems.

Self-monitoring begins with a rationale that emphasizes the importance of a personal scientist model of learning to observe one's own reactions. Then, clients are trained to use objective terms and anchors rather than affective-laden terms. For example, clients with panic disorder are trained to record the intensity of their symptoms on 0 to 10 point scales in place of using a general description of how "bad" the panic attack felt. The objectivity of recording is presumed to enhance its effectiveness. Then, clients are taught what, when, where, and how to record. Various types of recording exist, but the most common are event recording, or whether an event occurs during a period of recording (e.g., did a panic attack occur today), and frequency recording, or recording every event during the period of recording (e.g., every panic attack during the day).

Diaries are the most common form of recording, although counters or palm tops can be used. Data are then transformed into graphs, to demonstrate change over time (such as frequency of panic attacks per week, or average number of calories consumed per day). Feedback from the therapist about self-monitoring positively influences compliance with self-monitoring. In addition, therapists can use the self-monitoring data to emphasize progress or to identify previously undetailed functional relations among cognitions, behaviors, and emotions that are worthy of targeting in treatment.

The underlying mechanisms of self-monitoring are not entirely clear, although increased awareness of the problem behavior and/or its antecedents and consequences may facilitate motivation to change (Heidt & Marx, 2003). Additionally, recording the frequency of behaviors over the course of therapy may provide reinforcement as positive behavioral changes are noted. Also, self-monitoring may provide a cue or reminder for engaging in newly acquired cognitive and behavioral skills.

Rarely is there an outright contraindication to self-monitoring, although the method of monitoring is often modified to suit particular needs and offset potential pitfalls. For example, the person with obsessive–compulsive or perfectionistic tendencies may benefit from limit setting or tightly abbreviated forms of self-monitoring. Occasionally, negative affect can be worsened as it is monitored. For example, monitoring negative affect may activate negative self-evaluation; something that may be then addressed by cognitive restructuring of the negative self-evaluation. Self-monitoring in general will be more difficult for the person who lacks motivation and in turn serves to "confirm" a sense of failure in those persons who already judge themselves to be failures and cannot even succeed at self-monitoring (Heidt & Marx, 2003). In the latter case, problem solving and behavioral activation may be helpful approaches for increasing engagement in self-monitoring.

Relaxation

Relaxation has been a mainstay of behavioral treatments and encompasses an array of strategies, including autogenic training (Schultz & Luthe, 1959), progressive muscle relaxation training (Jacobson, 1938), breathing retraining (e.g., Kraft & Hoogduin, 1984), and various forms of meditation and yoga. Progressive muscle relaxation is a commonly used methodology, although in its condensed form of 8 to 15 sessions as standardized by Bernstein and Borkovec (1973) relative to the lengthy training (30–50 sessions) originally developed by Jacobson (1938). Progressive muscle relaxation training involves tensing and relaxing major muscle groups in progression, followed by deepening relaxation through slow breathing and/or imagery. The data show that muscle relaxation is anxiety reducing overall (e.g., Lang, Melamed & Hart, 1970). Relaxation has been used for sleep disturbance, headache, hypertension, asthma, alcohol usage, hyperactivity, and various forms of anxiety, as well as other disorders.

The procedure involves progressive tensing (for 10s) and relaxing (for 15–20s) the following muscle groups: dominant hand and forearm, dominant biceps, nondominant hand and forearm, nondominant biceps, forehead, upper cheeks and nose, lower cheeks and jaws, neck and throat, chest/shoulders and upper back, abdominal region, dominant thigh, dominant calf, dominant foot, nondominant thigh, nondominant calf, nondominant foot.

After a rationale is provided, the client's current emotional state is measured for purpose of comparison with the state that is achieved after relaxation. This can be done using a simple 0 to 100 visual analogue scale or a more sophisticated behavioral relaxation scale (Poppen, 1998). The latter scale also provides a precise definition of the targeted state of each body area to be achieved during relaxation. Next, the therapist provides a verbal description and then models the relaxed and tensed postures for each muscle area. The client then imitates the therapist while the latter provides feedback. The entire set of tensing and relaxing exercises are completed with therapist guidance. The client then practices the procedure daily between therapy sessions. Over sessions, the number of muscle groups can be reduced (from 16 to 8 to 4 muscle groups). Furthermore, cue-controlled relaxation is sometimes used, in which the state of relaxation between each tensing is paired with the word "relax"; that word then becomes a conditional cue that eventually elicits conditional relaxed sensations in isolation of the entire set of tensing and releasing exercises.

One mechanism underlying relaxation training is enhanced discrimination between feelings of relaxation and tension, achieved through paying attention to the sensations associated with each state during the training. The assumption is that clients then are better able to detect tension in their daily lives (Ferguson, 2003). Second, the training is presumed to build a skill for how to evoke the relaxation response as a means of self-control when experiencing tension in daily life. The physiological intent is for relaxation to activate more parasympathetic activity and thereby slow sympathetic autonomic processes such as heart rate and sweating. However, as with other relaxation techniques, such as breathing retraining, the mechanism may pertain more to a sense of control or other cognitive variables than to actual physiological change (e.g., Garssen, de Ruiter, & van Dyck, 1992).

When relaxation is paired with a biofeedback signal, as is used in the treatment of headache or chronic pain, another mechanism is brought to bear, that being shaping through reinforcement. That is, changes in physiological responding are achieved by continuous raising of the criterion (such as larger reductions in muscle tension) and reinforcement for each successful attainment of the criterion in the form of the biofeedback signal. Again, however, others suggest that perceptions of control may be equally if not more accountable for the effectiveness of biofeedback, since use of bogus biofeedback signals is as effective as veridical feedback (e.g., Rains, 2008). As an example, Mary had suffered from chronic tension headaches for many years. She was first taught progressive muscle relaxation training, including cue-controlled relaxation, which she practiced twice daily in relaxing environments for three weeks. Then, while continuing to use progressive muscle relaxation as a daily exercise, she simultaneously used the cue-controlled element of relaxation within the context of six weekly biofeedback sessions as she learned to progressively lower her muscle tension. As a result of this training, Mary's self-monitoring of headache activity indicated that it had decreased by approximately one half since the two weeks before treatment initiated.

The skill of relaxation is most often employed for states of heightened autonomic arousal that interfere with quality of life or therapy progress, or as a coping skill to actively face challenging situations. Relaxation has been shown to be particularly helpful in the treatment of phobias and anxiety disorders, preparing for surgery and other medical procedures, and coping with chronic pain. It is also incorporated into treatments that focus on emotion regulation, as in dialectical behavior therapy for borderline personality disorder (Linehan, 1994). Occasionally, negative reactions can be produced by relaxation, such as relaxation-induced anxiety (Heide & Borkovec, 1983).

The latter involves intrusive thoughts, fears of losing control, and the experience of unusual and therefore anxiety-producing bodily sensations (such as depersonalization). However, rather than being a contraindication to continued relaxation, discussion of the processes and continued exposure to relaxation and its associated states can be an effective tool for managing relaxation-induced anxiety.

Behavioral Rehearsal of Social Skills and Assertiveness

In behavioral rehearsal of social skills and assertiveness, a set of skills is taught through instruction, modeling, and role play and feedback, as therapist and client play out different roles. Social skills include nonverbal (e.g., facial expressions, body movements, affective displays) as well as verbal components (e.g., refusing requests from others that seem unreasonable, and making requests; Dow, 1994).

An initial step is evaluation of skills in social and assertive situations, usually complementing the client's self-report by observational methodology, such as through role plays with the therapist or direct observation of client behaviors in the natural environment. A rationale then is provided that emphasizes how learning social and assertive skills will help clients to achieve personal control and respect for self and others, which in turn will contribute to the attainment of their own life goals. A hierarchy of behaviors is then devised for the purposes of role playing and behavioral rehearsal. For example, assertive requests for behavior change in others include a statement of the negative impact of the current behavior, provision of a specific and reasonable alternative behavior, and a statement of the likely positive impact of the new behavior on both parties.

Then, the therapist directly models the specific skill or presents the skill through another model, such as through the use of video. Modeling can involve a mastery approach, in which the model performs the desired behavior with confidence and competency. Alternatively, modeling can involve a coping approach, in which the model initially displays some trepidation and error followed by increasing skill. The latter approach may be particularly helpful for clients who are hesitant or fearful (e.g., Naugle & Maher, 2003). The client then rehearses the behavior.[1] Typically, clients are asked to evaluate their own performance first before the therapist reinforces their efforts, provides verbal feedback regarding execution of the skill, and shapes behavioral approximations. Videotaping sometimes can be helpful in this regard. Following mastery in-session, homework is assigned to practice the new behaviors in real-life situations between treatment sessions. Consideration also is given to realistic performance expectations and the value of self-reinforcement for continued rehearsal and practice.

A subset of social skills training is communication training for couples in distress. The assumption is that either couples lack the communication skills for negotiating conflict, and/or for reasons of stimulus control of behaviors, effective communication skills are not being used in the context of interpersonal tension. Couples communication training involves speaker/listener skills to understand and validate the partner's perspective. The therapist defines each skill. Listening skills include parroting (i.e., repeat), paraphrasing (i.e., rephrase), reflection (i.e., discern emotional meaning of speaker's message), and validation (i.e., convey that speaker's message is understandable). Speaking skills include learning to make succinct statements, to clarify and express accurate feeling statements, and to level (i.e., to express the core underlying feelings associated with a problem) (e.g., Gottman et al., 1976). Then, the therapist provides reinforcement and corrective feedback to the couple as each practice using these skills to communicate in the therapy setting. Homework is to practice the same skills in their daily life between sessions.

In terms of mechanisms, behavioral rehearsal itself relies on principles of reinforcement and shaping. The new behavior is reinforced by the therapist. Once achieved, skills of communication and assertiveness may function as reciprocal inhibitors of conditional fear in social situations and/or contribute to extinction of CRs by devaluing the expectancy of the US (i.e., increased assertiveness lessens fear of negative reactions from others). Additionally, the same skills may function to overcome deficits in

---

[1] There are some occasions when modeling and overt rehearsal are not appropriate, such as when addressing skills associated with sexual intimacy; in these cases, covert or imaginal rehearsal is used instead.

behavioral repertoires (e.g., McFall & Marston, 1970). The new or modified behaviors are expected to result in an increase in positive reinforcers and decrease in punishers from the social environment, thereby improving overall mood and life satisfaction and functioning. Finally, implementation of these newly acquired skills may raise self-efficacy and decrease negative beliefs about oneself and the world.

Behavioral rehearsal of social skills and assertiveness is particularly helpful when there are clear deficits in these skills (e.g., pervasive developmental disorders, psychosis, or extreme social anxiety or avoidant personality disorder), or their rate of expression is limited overall or limited in certain contexts (due to anxiety or depression, for example). Assertiveness training should be implemented in a culturally responsive manner. This involves consideration of cultural values pertaining to independence and autonomy. CBT in general and assertiveness training in particular is permeated with European/North American norms that place high value on independence and autonomy (see Hays & Iwamasa, 2006). Assertiveness may conflict with values of collectivism and the importance of family in Asian, Arabic, Latino, African American, and other cultures. Culturally sensitive modifications to assertiveness include prefacing assertive communication with traditional forms of deference and respect (e.g., Organista, 2006), or by replacing assertiveness with other CBT strategies, such as problem solving.

Problem-Solving Training

Problem solving is a skill that has been implemented for a wide array of difficulties, including anxiety, depression, couples conflict, and stress management. In general, clients are taught a set of skills for approaching problems of everyday living. Steps involved in problem solving include problem definition and formulation, generation of alternatives, decision making, and verification.

D'Zurilla and Nezu (1999) identified two main targets of treatment: the orientation toward problem solving and the style of problem solving. The goals of problem-solving training are to increase positive and decrease negative *problem-solving orientation* and to foster a rational problem-solving style that minimizes maladaptive styles of being impulsive or careless or avoiding problems. Thus, training begins with steps of problem-solving orientation to develop positive self-efficacy beliefs, such as by reverse-advocacy role play that encourages clients to recognize their overly negative beliefs through contrast and by visualization of successfully resolving a problem and being reinforced as a result. The orientation phase also includes recognition that problems are a normal part of human existence and ways of identifying problems as they occur, such as by using negative emotions as a cue for recognizing that a problem exists and to observe what is occurring in the environment that is causing the emotions.

For the *style of problem solving phase*, clients are first trained in problem definition. This involves gathering information about the problem, objectively and concisely defining the problem, separating facts from assumptions, identifying the features that make the situation problematic, and setting realistic goals (Nezu, Nezu, & Lombardo, 2003). Next, alternatives are developed by generating as many solutions as possible, deferring judgment until a full list is generated, and then developing a list of action plans for the enactment of each solution. In the decision-making phase, a cost benefit analysis is conducted of each solution to identify the ones that are most likely to be successful and to be implemented. Effective solutions, or solutions that are likely to be successful and lead to the most positive and least negative consequences, are then selected. The final step is implementing the action plan associated with the most effective solution, and evaluating the success of its implementation along with troubleshooting and modification where necessary.

Problem solving is essentially a skill-building intervention. The mechanisms underlying problem solving include reinforcement from skills acquisition and from the success with which the problem solving resolves pending problems. In addition, by facing problematic situations rather than avoiding them, a type of exposure is being conducted that may lead to extinction of CRs. Furthermore, changes in cognitive appraisals and assumptions are involved in the problem orientation phase of the procedure. Also, successful implementation of problem solving may raise self-efficacy and provide evidence that disconfirms negative beliefs about the self and the world.

As an example, John, a writer, was suffering from depression. One of the problem behaviors connected with his depression, both as a cause and consequence, was incompletion of writing projects. He had almost a dozen half-written short stories and scripts and had not completed a writing project for several years. This in turn was causing financial problems, as writing was his primary source of income. Treatment began by specifying the problem as incompletion of writing projects, with a clear description of the factors that appeared to contribute to incompletion, such as poor time management. A realistic goal was set of completing the project that was the closest to being finished within 4 weeks. Next, John began brainstorming solutions, including finding a writing buddy; scheduling his time more effectively; providing reinforcements for each interval in which writing was accomplished; removing all other writing projects from his desk to increase focus upon the selected project; paying someone to help him write; taking a 4-week retreat to a place where he would be less distracted; and asking his family to leave for 4 weeks so he would be less distracted. The steps involved in each potential solution were also generated. For example, to schedule his time more effectively, John needed to prioritize his writing within the context of his other daily responsibilities as a father and husband, schedule several blocks of time per day for writing only, and learn how to communicate the importance of this schedule to his family. He then considered which solutions were most feasible and most likely to succeed. He selected scheduling his time more effectively and providing reinforcement (a phone call to a friend, or reading, among other reinforcers), for each time he wrote for the scheduled period of time. This plan was put into practice. After the first week, John realized that he had scheduled too many short blocks of time during the day and revised his plan to two 2-hour blocks of time. With that revision, John was able to complete his project in a timely manner.

Problem-solving training has been used widely across psychological disorders as well as for individuals with medical disorders, marital and family problems, and general stress management. Problem-solving training also has been found to be effective in primary care settings for the management of depression and is often incorporated with other cognitive and behavioral strategies such as when treating substance use disorders. There appear to be few contraindications to this approach, although it would not be the preferred approach when the evidence indicates that other approaches are more effective for specific disorders, as in the case of some anxiety disorders where repeated exposure to phobic stimuli is especially effective.

Behavioral Activation

Behavioral activation as a treatment for depression originated from instrumental conditioning models, in which depressed mood was attributed to proportionately more punishers than positive reinforcers. As a way of counteracting this disproportionate reinforcement schedule, Lewinsohn and colleagues (e.g., Lewinsohn, 1974) encouraged increased access to positive reinforcers by using activity logs and activity scheduling from a standard list of activities to increase engagement in pleasant activities. More recently, Jacobson and colleagues (Jacobson, Martell, & Dimidjian, 2001) took a more idiographic approach to identifying the types of activities that would increase positive reinforcement by relying on a functional analysis for a given individual. They also emphasized the importance of behavioral activation as a way of countering avoidance of life challenges and associated negative emotions. Such avoidance is presumed to contribute to ongoing depression. For example, requesting to speak to one's boss to make amends for an error made at work would serve as an activity that counters avoidance of the negative emotions anticipated to arise during the interaction with the boss. By this kind of emphasis on counteracting avoidance, behavioral activation overlaps with problem solving and with exposure therapy for anxiety disorders.

Behavioral activation begins with a functional analysis of the antecedents and maintainers of the lack of behavior, which informs the way to structure behavioral activation in a given individual's context. A functional analysis is essential since the same behavior, or lack thereof, may serve a very different function for different people. For example, arranging to have coffee with friends may be an adaptive socialization, or a maladaptive avoidance of other responsibilities. Understanding the context of depression includes broadly assessing significant life events, and ways in which behavior has altered since being depressed, as well as the methods that have been used to cope with depression that may be in themselves problematic (e.g., avoidance behaviors). This information is then used for a conceptualization of the life events that have contributed to depression by making the client's life less rewarding and ways in which attempts to cope with depression by avoidance have contributed to depression.

Activity charts then are used to assess current levels of activity and the connections between activity and mood, and to help clients monitor avoidance behaviors as well as steps that are being taken toward accomplishing stated life goals (Martell, 2003). Clients then are encouraged to become aware of their own avoidant strategies and to choose between continuing to be avoidant and depressed or to engage in activities that will eventually lead to improved mood. An acronym ACTION is used to help clients assess when they are being avoidant:

Assess – is my behavior avoidant?
Choose – whether to activate or continue to avoid.
Try – the chosen behavior.
Integrate – new activity into regular routine.
Observe – the outcome; does the new behavior lift mood or life situation?
Never – give up. (Martell, 2003)

The purported mechanisms underlying behavioral activation are that by increasing activity and blocking avoidance, clients come into contact with more natural positive reinforcers from their environment. Also, behavioral activation establishes a regular routine and encourages functionality. Furthermore, behavioral activation helps clients learn to become active even when they feel they cannot possibly complete tasks or get any pleasure from life (Martell, 2003). By encouraging approach to previously avoided situations, behavioral activation may contribute to the extinction of CRs. Also, self-efficacy may be effectively raised and in turn contribute to further motivation for behavioral activation. Finally, although behavioral activation treatment does not attempt to change the content of cognition, performance accomplishment is likely to provide evidence that disconfirms overly negative appraisals about the self and the world.

Behavioral activation was developed specifically for the treatment of depression. There are no clear contraindications for the person who is depressed, with the exception of situations in which activating the client may place them at risk of harm due to an abusive partner or violent living circumstances (Martell, 2003). Given the contextual basis of behavioral activation, in which the goal is to encourage clients to look "outward at their life context rather than at hypothesized internal defects" (Martell, 2003, p. 29), behavioral activation is not usually combined with a cognitive therapy focus on the content of negative cognitions. Instead, cognitions are addressed in terms of their function, such as by evaluating where and when these negative cognitions occur and what is the effect of the cognition on what the person feels and does next. Then, the treatment refocuses on how to behave differently, in a way that is not guided by the negative cognitions. In certain cultural contexts, behavioral activation may be modified to include activities with family members.

Behavioral Contracting

Another strategy driven by reinforcement principles is behavioral contracting, or contingency contracting. Simply, this represents a statement of a set of behaviors to be followed, and related positive and negative consequences to be carried out conditionally on compliance or noncompliance with the plan. As such, it is the direct translation of the principles described previously for instrumental learning theory. Behavioral contracting has been applied in complement with other cognitive and behavioral strategies, in CBT packages (e.g, problem-solving therapy), across a wide array of disorders, including family-marital problems, substance use disorders, weight loss, smoking cessation, and physical exercise. Aside from targeting specific behavioral excesses or deficits, behavioral contracting can be used as a tool to facilitate compliance with CBT. For example, behavioral contracting may be used to enhance engagement in exposure therapy, behavioral activation, or response prevention.

Contracting depends on an initial functional analysis that indicates the antecedents and consequences of current behavioral patterns and that suggests ways for modifying antecedents and/or alternative consequences necessary to initiate and maintain behavioral changes. The ways of altering antecedents and consequences were described previously, including removing or modifying antecedents, changing establishing operations, and delivering consequences. A set of parameters determine the effectiveness of a positive or negative consequence for a behavior and should be taken into account when designing behavioral contracts. These include its relative size or significance, the immediacy with which it is delivered, and the consistency of delivery. Consistency is particularly important during the phase of acquisition of a new behavior, whereas ratio schedules of reinforcement are more effective for maintaining a new behavior once it is acquired (see Martin & Pear, 2003).

The critical steps to behavioral contracting have been summarized by Houmanfar, Maglieri, and Roman (2003) as the following: clearly specified and reasonable short-term and long-term goals; clearly specified target behaviors for change, and the conditions under which the target behavior will occur; a monitoring system to establish whether the target behavioral goals are being met; and clearly specified reward contingencies for compliance and consequences for noncompliance. Furthermore, the negotiated contract is to be agreed upon and signed by all participants.

The primary underlying mechanism of behavioral contracting is operant conditioning—the reinforcement of desired behaviors and punishment of undesired behaviors. Successful behavioral change may also raise self-efficacy and serve to disconfirm negative appraisals about oneself and the world that in turn motivate continued behavioral change.

As an example, a client with obsessive compulsive hoarding contracts to discard magazines and newspapers from the living room of his house for 15 minutes each day, just before dinner time, in order to achieve the long-term goal of clearing out his living room. Upon completion of the 15 minutes each day, the client agrees to reward himself by either watching the 10 o'clock news or having dessert after dinner. If the target goal is not met, then the client will neither watch the news nor have dessert. Progress is monitored by a daily log of number of minutes spent discarding materials.

Problems with behavioral contracts can arise when they are too restrictive, appear to be punishing, or are too rigid and do not allow for client input (Houmanfar, Maglieri, & Roman, 2003). Vagueness of the contract, lack of therapist attention to the contract, and lack of encouragement to apply the relevant contingencies may all hinder effectiveness as well. Finally, behavioral contracting is typically not employed directly as an intervention for skill-based behavioral deficits (such as lack of social skills), although it can be used as a tool for encouraging engagement in skill-based behavioral acquisition.

As with CBT in general, behavioral contracting in particular emphasizes change, and such an emphasis can be at odds with cultural influences that restrict the client's ability to create and implement change (see Hays & Iwamasa, 2006). Thus, contracting for behavioral changes should take cultural and interpersonal constraints into account and be modified accordingly. For example, a behavioral contract designed to increase physical exercise schedules physical activities at times that do not overlap with familial activities so that behavioral change goals do not conflict with familial goals.

Habit Reversal

Habit reversal was first developed by Azrin and Nunn (1974) for nervous habits and tics, based on the theory that such behaviors persist because of response chaining, limited awareness, excessive practice, and social tolerance. Nowadays, habit reversal is used for tics as well as trichotillomania and a range of repetitive behaviors that are controlled by "automatic reinforcement," or self-stimulatory behaviors (e.g., hair pulling).

The treatment begins with a detailed analysis of the sequence of behaviors involved in the habit and the antecedents and consequences. Then, awareness training is initiated, in which clients are reinforced for detecting the first signs of a particular behavioral habit so that eventually they will be able to interrupt the habit early in the sequence. This includes awareness of the environmental as well as covert antecedents (e.g., specific sensations in the area affected by a motor or verbal tic). Awareness training is practiced in session with natural or simulated habits and is reinforced by the therapist. Next, in competing response training, clients learn to perform a competing response that is inconspicuous, requires little effort, and competes physically with the habit. For example, a competing response for a vocal tic is diaphragmatic breathing with the mouth closed, and a competing response for nail biting is to apply hand lotion. These competing responses are practiced in session with natural or simulated habits and again combined with therapist reinforcement. Clients are then instructed to use the competing response in their daily lives either when the antecedents are present or early in the chain of behaviors.

Habit reversal is a skill-based intervention that rests heavily on principles of reinforcement. Specifically, attempts are made to block the positive reinforcement (usually sensory) associated with enacting the repetitive behavior, by replacing it with a competing behavior. Sometimes therapist reinforcement for implementing the competing response is accompanied by social reinforcement from significant others for not engaging in the repetitive behavior. Response generalization also is involved, via imagining successful control of the habit in situations where it had been a problem. Also, successful control of a repetitive behavior is likely to increase self-efficacy, which in turn motivates continued efforts to control the behavior. These strategies may also lead to more positive appraisals about the self that in turn contribute to motivation for continued habit reversal practice.

Habit reversal was developed specifically to manage repetitive behaviors such as tics, hair pulling, stuttering, nail biting, teeth grinding, skin picking and scratching, and self-biting. It is most appropriate for behaviors that are controlled by automatic reinforcement, or self-stimulatory behaviors. It is not appropriate for repetitive behaviors that are controlled by consequences of escape from an aversive situation (e.g., such as compulsive behaviors that lead to reduction in distress or attenuation of an obsession) or positive social consequences.

Exposure-Based Strategies

Exposure Therapy

Exposure therapy developed directly from the principles of extinction of classically conditioned responses. It is most frequently used for anxiety disorders but is sometimes incorporated into treatments for substance use disorders, eating disorders and other disorders. Exposure therapy involves systematic and repeated approach to either phobic stimuli or stimuli that produce craving, without reinforcement by an aversive or appetitive US, so that eventually these stimuli lose their capacity to produce a CR of either fear or craving. The stimuli encompass external cues, such as agoraphobic situations or drugs and drug paraphernalia, as well as internal cues, such as feared bodily sensations associated with panic attacks, memories of trauma, obsessions, catastrophic images, or drug cravings.

Wolpe's (1958) *systematic desensitization* combines relaxation with exposure to feared stimuli. Systematic desensitization represented the first application of conditioning principles to the treatment of fear and anxiety disorders. As originally developed, systematic desensitization is conducted in imagination. Imagining fearful stimuli was assumed to be equivalent to actually confronting fearful stimuli in real life. Relaxation was included to compete with and inhibit the anxiety response. For this reason, it is important that the relaxation response is stronger than the anxiety response; hence Wolpe decided to conduct systematic desensitization using a graded exposure format so that anxiety levels are maintained at relatively low levels. Images of feared stimulus are organized into a hierarchy from least to most anxiety provoking; desensitization begins with the least anxiety-provoking image and then gradually moves up the hierarchy to more anxiety-provoking images. By so doing, success at each earlier step on the hierarchy is assumed to lessen anxiety for the subsequent steps on the hierarchy.

After hierarchy generation, systematic desensitization proceeds by first presenting a neutral scene, followed by repeated pairing of the least anxiety-evoking image from the hierarchy with subsequent relaxation. Clients are asked to imagine, signal (e.g., raise their hand) when the image is clear, and continue imagining for a specified period of time, after which the level of anxiety is rated and relaxation is practiced. This pairing is repeated the number of times necessary until the hierarchy item can be imagined with minimal or no anxiety, at which point the next item on the hierarchy is imagined. In its original form, imagining of fearful scenes was limited to no more than 15 seconds (usually 5–7 seconds) or until anxiety was felt, whichever came sooner, at which point there was a return to the relaxation state. Goldfried (1971) developed a self-control version of desensitization. Instead of removing the image and returning to a relaxed state, the client is encouraged to maintain the image and practice relaxation to remove tensions and anxiety. In this version, desensitization is viewed as an opportunity to rehearse coping skills.

Wolpe (1958) emphasized the mechanism of counterconditioning through reciprocal inhibition. He drew from the work of Sherrington (1947), who established that if one group of muscles is stimulated, then an antagonistic muscle group is inhibited, a process he called *reciprocal inhibition*. Wolpe extended this principle to anxiety and stated that when a response antagonistic to anxiety can be made to occur in the presence of anxiety-provoking stimuli and results in a complete or partial suppression of the anxiety response, then the bond between the stimulus and the anxiety response is weakened. Thus, in systematic desensitization, individuals progress gradually through increasingly more anxiety-provoking imagined encounters with phobic stimuli while using relaxation as a reciprocal inhibitor of rising anxiety.

However, the premises of reciprocal inhibition were challenged by evidence showing that graduated imaginal exposure to feared situations was equally effective whether combined with relaxation training or not (see Craske et al., 2008, for a review). Also, when relaxation did enhance the efficacy of imaginal systematic desensitization, its effectiveness was attributed to enhanced vividness of imagery, which was associated with *increased* autonomic arousal rather than the intended purpose of relaxation of inducing a relaxed physiological response that was antagonistic to anxious arousal (Craske et al., 2008).

Thus, the field moved away from relying on relaxation to counter condition anxiety. Nowadays, exposure is conducted in a number of ways. One way is to use imagination, as in systematic desensitization, but without relaxation. Imaginal exposure is most appropriate for stimuli that are difficult to practice confronting in real life (such as air travel) or are inherently imaginal (such as obsessions in the case of obsessive compulsive disorder or memories of trauma in posttraumatic stress disorder). Another modality gaining popularity is virtual reality, a strength of which is the control it provides over the parameters of exposure. For example, in the treatment of public speaking, virtual reality can provide systematic exposure to different sized audiences, different responses from audiences, and so on. Writing exposure is sometimes used for exposure to traumas in the treatment of posttraumatic stress disorder. In vivo, or real-life, exposure is commonly used for most anxiety disorders. For example, individuals with social anxiety are exposed to social situations as are persons with agoraphobia exposed to situations such as driving or being away from home. Interoceptive exposure involves repeated and systematic exposure to feared bodily sensations, most applicable to panic disorder (e.g., repeated hyperventilation to overcome fears of sensations of shortness of breath and parasthesias). Different modalities of exposure often are combined. For example, writing exposure or imaginal exposure to memories of a trauma can be combined with in vivo exposure to situational reminders of the trauma. Similarly, imaginal exposure to obsessions is usually accompanied by in vivo exposure to obsessional triggers, and virtual reality to phobic situations is usually accompanied by instructions to practice exposure in real-life situations as well.

During exposure, clients usually are encouraged to experience the full emotional response elicited without engaging in overt and more subtle forms of avoidance. In addition, safety signals are gradually removed, since, as described previously, safety signals are believed to undermine corrective learning during exposure. Exposure is conducted in session under the direction of the therapist who gives guidance, feedback, and reinforcement. Sometimes the therapist models in vivo (and/or interoceptive exposure, which is especially helpful when clients are hesitant about performing the exposure task, or when clients have not acquired the skills required to be able to conduct the exposure (such as how to approach and touch a particular animal). In this case, the therapist models and then the client imitates. Therapist-directed exposures in session are followed by self-directed exposures between sessions. When it is not practical for in vivo exposure to be conducted under the supervision of the therapist, the therapist and client jointly design an in vivo exposure task. Clients then imaginally rehearse the in vivo exposure in session before attempting the in vivo exposure task on their own, between sessions. The client reports back at the next session for a collaborative review of what was learned and how to structure the next exposure practice. Sometimes significant others, such as parents or partners, are involved as coaches for exposure practices conducted between sessions.

In the context of anxiety, exposure can be conducted gradually to progressively more anxiety-provoking situations or as flooding exposure, meaning prolonged and continuous exposure to highly anxiety-provoking stimuli. A few studies have shown flooding exposure to be as effective as graduated exposure, at least in those willing to undertake intense exposure (e.g., Miller, 2002), although further comparative research is needed. Flooding therapy is commonly used in exposure to traumatic images for posttraumatic stress disorder and obsessional content in obsessive compulsive disorder, and it is sometimes used for in vivo exposure to feared situations for panic disorder and agoraphobia. Flooding exposure typically elicits high levels of physiological arousal and subjective distress, at least during the initial phases of exposure.

Parameters used to determine the length of each exposure practice for anxiety disorders have varied over the years. Proponents of emotional processing theory (Foa & Kozak, 1986), which is described later in this chapter, recommend that exposure trials continue for the duration required until fear declines, since fear decline is evidence for corrective learning. However, with the more recent recognition that diminution of the expression of fear in a given exposure practice is not necessarily a sign of corrective learning (Craske et al., 2008), we have recommended a shift from "stay in the situation until fear has declined" to "stay in the situation until you have learned what you need to learn, and sometimes that means learning that you can tolerate fear."

Exposure therapy is sometimes conducted in conjunction with coping tools, such as relaxation[2] or slowed breathing, cognitive restructuring, or imagery rescripting. These coping tools are intended to increase willingness to engage in exposure therapy as well as to facilitate its effectiveness. As an example, individuals with agoraphobia may be taught a method of slow diaphragmatic breathing and helped to generate a set of coping self-statements as tools to be used to manage excessive levels of anxiety as they walk through a busy shopping mall. However, as described in more

---

[2] Use of relaxation as a coping tool differs from relaxation as a counterconditioner in systematic desensitization in that the former is taught as a general method for lowering anxiety as exposure is conducted, whereas in the latter case, the application of relaxation is precisely tied to ongoing levels of anxiety with a continuous shifting back and forth between the imagined fear scene and relaxation.

detail in a later section, the degree to which these tools actually enhance the efficacy of exposure therapy is unclear.

Following the contradictions to Wolpe's model of reciprocal inhibition, habituation was evoked by researchers in the 1960s and 1970s (e.g., Watts, 1971) as an explanatory process for systematic desensitization. Habituation refers simply to reduction in response strength with repeated stimulus presentations. However, habituation is traditionally viewed as a transient process, since dishabituation (or increased response strength) usually follows habituation. Consequently, habituation is unlikely to account for long-lasting effects from exposure therapy.

The concept of habituation was combined with the concept of corrective learning to explain the effects of exposure therapy for fear and anxiety in the widely known emotional processing theory (EPT) put forth by Foa and Kozak (1986). The theory was subsequently revised in 1996 by Foa and McNally. EPT purports that the effects of exposure therapy derive from activation of a "fear structure" and integration of information that is incompatible with it, resulting in the development of a non-fear structure that replaces or competes with the original. A fear structure, as first posited by Lang (1971), is a set of propositions about a stimulus, response, and their meaning that are stored in memory. For example, a fear structure associated with fears of spiders might involve a stimulus proposition of big spiders, a response proposition of a racing heart and stomach upset, and a meaning proposition of being poisoned by the spider. The index of activation is fear, measured subjectively and physiologically.

Once activated, corrective learning is purported to occur through integration of information that is incompatible with the structure. Incompatible information is presumed to derive from two primary sources. The first is within-session habituation of the physiological and/or verbalized fear response (i.e., reduction from the start to the end of an exposure session) that disassociates the stimulus from response propositions (i.e., the stimulus is no longer connected with fear responding). Within-session habituation is considered to be a necessary prerequisite for between-session habituation over repeated occasions of exposure (i.e., reduction in peak anxiety from the first to the last exposure session). Between-session habituation is purported to form the basis for long-term learning and to be mediated by changes in the meaning proposition, in the form of lowered probability of harm (i.e., risk) and lessened negativity (i.e., valence) of the stimulus. EPT clearly guided clinicians to the view the level of fear expressed throughout exposure as a sign of learning. Hence, clinicians conducting exposure therapy were guided to help clients remain in the feared situation until their fear declined. However, there is little evidence that within-session habituation plays a role in the overall outcomes from exposure therapy, and hence questions are now being raised about the premises of EPT (Craske et al., 2008).

We recently suggested that exposure therapy works by generating new sets of expectancies that inhibit the original fear-based expectancies. It follows, then, that exposure therapy is best structured in a way that maximally disconfirms the expectancy for negative outcomes or contributes to inhibitory expectancies that negative outcomes will not occur or are not as negative as expected (Craske et al., 2008). For example, a woman fears fainting when driving and fully expects that she will faint if she drives more than 5 miles from home. In this case, exposure to driving more than 5 miles from home would be the optimal way of disconfirming her expectancy of fainting. If the exposure were to driving less than 5 miles from home, her expectancies about fainting may remain unchanged. Clearly, this approach requires a careful analysis of expectancies. If the aversive event is fear itself, as is often the case in anxiety disorders, then exposure trials would be designed to last longer than the interval of time (or number of repetitions) at which fear is judged to become intolerable. This approach to exposure therapy differs very much from the habituation model that encourages staying in the exposure until the fear declines. Instead, it is more consistent with cognitive appraisal theories that view exposure therapy as a means for gathering data to disconfirm misappraisals. In cognitive therapy, we call this *behavioral experimentation*. However, in contrast to cognitive appraisal models, which target conscious cognitions, we (Craske et al., 2008) propose that the new inhibitory expectancies may develop implicitly through the experience of the exposure.

Exposure therapy does not teach skills and therefore is not appropriate when anxiety is directly related to skill deficits, as sometimes occurs in social anxiety or phobias of certain situations that require skills (e.g., fear of swimming in the ocean in someone who has not learned how to swim). Since exposure typically evokes high levels of anxiety at some point, it is generally not recommended when there are complicating medical conditions that make high levels of autonomic arousal potentially harmful (e.g., certain arrythmias or severe asthma); systematic desensitization may be considered under these conditions. Because of the potential for high levels of anxiety, attrition is a concern, especially if attrition occurs after initial exposure and before the benefits of exposure have taken place; attrition following brief exposure may be sensitizing. Thus, careful attention is given to the rationale for exposure and readiness for exposure. Also, surrounding reinforcers for avoidant behavior (e.g., attention from a significant other for agoraphobic avoidance) may serve to counteract the aims of exposure therapy and should be evaluated and addressed where appropriate to minimize inadvertent sabotaging. Another contraindication is when the exposure is to situations that are actually harmful, such as exposure to an abuser. Also, exposure may be contraindicated for persons with psychosis, other thought disorders or dementias, especially when behavioral avoidance of certain situations is adaptive for them. In contrast to behavioral activation, exposure therapy can be readily combined with cognitive therapy.

Response Prevention

Response prevention refers to blocking avoidance behaviors in general, including safety signals and safety-seeking behaviors, although the specific methodology is most closely tied to the blocking of compulsive behavior in the treatment of obsessive compulsive disorder. Basically, clients are prevented from carrying out their usual compulsive rituals as they confront their obsessions or obsessional triggers. The procedure was originated by Meyer in 1966, and Rachman and Hodgson (1980) who observed that when clients were exposed to obsessional cues and at the same time were prevented from engaging in rituals, their anxiety eventually declined. This observation encouraged the combination of exposure therapy with response prevention in the treatment of obsessive compulsive disorder. For example, clients may be asked to touch an object that is perceived as being contaminated, such as a door handle, and then prevent themselves from washing their hands. The research indicates that the combination of exposure and response prevention is superior to exposure alone for obsessive compulsive disorder (e.g., Foa, Steketee, Grayson, Turner, & Latimer, 1984).

The method of response prevention begins with establishing the functional relations between obsessions and compulsions, with careful attention to covert as well as overt compulsions. Examples of overt compulsions are cleaning and checking appliances or locks, whereas covert compulsions include mentally reviewing actions over the past week or thinking specific words or phrases. Next, clients are given a treatment rationale for preventing compulsions in response to obsessions. Care is taken to distinguish prevention of compulsions from attempts to prevent obsessions, since the latter is counterproductive. Then, exposure and response prevention is initiated.

In its earliest form, response prevention was implemented in an inpatient setting with continual supervision by nursing staff who literally prevented clients from carrying out rituals. However, simply instructing clients to relinquish rituals is almost as effective, at least for less-severe compulsions. Response prevention can be done completely or gradually. An example of complete response prevention for compulsions of excessive washing would be no washing at all for an entire week. However, complete response prevention is difficult unless in a highly structured and supportive environment. In less-structured outpatient treatment settings, response prevention is more often done gradually (e.g., gradually reduce the number of minutes showering each day).

Response prevention is predicated on the functional relationship that exists between obsessions and compulsions—that obsessions evoke anxiety, and compulsions reduce anxiety. Habituation and reinforcement mechanisms are presumed to contribute to its effectiveness. That is, by preventing compulsions, habituation occurs to the obsession. Also, because compulsions tend to (but not always) alleviate anxiety, they are instrumentally reinforced and more likely to be repeated over time; preventing them interrupts this self-perpetuating cycle. Thus, the goal is for clients to learn that anxiety habituates without having to rely on compulsions, whereas engagement in compulsions maintains anxiety over the long term.

As such, response prevention may be more appropriately described as a reinforcement- and skill-based strategy than an extinction-based strategy. However, more recently, extinction mechanisms have been evoked as well, since by preventing the compulsion, clients learn that feared catastrophic events do not occur. For example, clients with obsessions of harming a loved one learn through exposure to the obsession and response prevention of compulsive behaviors that they do not actually harm their loved ones, and therefore new inhibitory expectancies are developed. In addition, accomplishment of exposure and response prevention is likely to raise self-efficacy. At the level of explicit cognitive appraisal, response prevention may also lead to less negative appraisals about the obsessions (e.g., "having the thought that I will do something obscene does not mean that I am obscene").

Although most often referred to in the context of compulsive behaviors, any kind of avoidance behavior can be response prevented within the context of exposure therapy for any anxiety disorder. Hence, reliance on safety signals or safety-seeking behaviors is typically response prevented. Thus, the same contraindications as outlined for exposure therapy apply to response prevention. In addition, it is generally agreed that full response prevention is more effective than partial response prevention, and yet full response prevention is more difficult to implement on an outpatient treatment basis. Consequently, severe obsessive–compulsive disorder may benefit from intensive, day treatment or inpatient settings where full response prevention can be more readily implemented. Also, family members can become involved in the treatment and encourage response prevention in the home environment, something that is particularly helpful for children with obsessive compulsive disorder.

Cognitive-Based Strategies

Three cognitive appraisal approaches are described, with the first two being more than a single strategy but rather an entire therapeutic approach. The mechanisms underlying these approaches were fully detailed in Chapter 3 and thus are not reviewed again here.

Rational–Emotive Behavior Therapy

Rational–emotive behavior therapists teach clients to directly dispute their irrational thoughts, although the precise steps through which this is done is less standardized than for many other behavioral and cognitive strategies. In general, the first step involves verbal persuasion aimed at convincing clients of the tenets of rational–emotive behavior therapy (REBT). Clients are helped to realize that it is not events themselves but appraisals and thinking styles that lead to emotional distress. They are educated about rational versus irrational beliefs, with the latter being characterized as rigid and extreme, inconsistent with social reality, illogical, prone to dysfunctional feelings, prone to dysfunctional behavioral consequences, demanding and "musturbatory," "awfulizing and terribilizing," and depreciative of human worth (Ellis, 2003). The next step is identification of idiosyncratic irrational thoughts through client self-monitoring and therapist feedback. Then, the therapist directly challenges irrational ideas and models rational reinterpretations of events. Disputation may involve questioning the evidence for the belief or the utility for holding the belief, questioning the catastrophic implications that have been drawn out about situations, or demonstrating through logic that the belief is illogical. Sometimes the focus is on the form rather than the content of cognition, such as when encouraging clients to change "must" statements into "would" statements. Verbal disputation is sometimes complemented with imaginal disputation and repeated cognitive rehearsal aimed at substituting rational self-statements for previously irrational ones.

These skills are intended to be internalized by clients, who are taught to identify their own irrational beliefs and to actively dispute them, through strategies such as asking where is the empirical evidence for a particular belief (e.g., "What is the evidence that one must perform well at all times?"). In addition, they are taught logical disputation (e.g., "Does it follow that if I want to do well then I have to do well?"); pragmatic or heuristic disputing (e.g., "Where will it get me if I keep demanding instead of preferring to do well?"); changing "musts" to "preferences"; and setting goals without raising them to unrealistic and illogical demands. Other strategies include rational coping statements, positive visualization, cost–benefit analyses, modeling, unconditional self-acceptance, and practical problem solving (Ellis, 2003). As can be seen, a number of different strategies are used in REBT, but the guiding principle of every strategy is to change irrational beliefs to more rational beliefs.

Homework assignments include self-monitoring of antecedents, beliefs, and consequences; attempts at disputation on one's own; and behavioral assignments to practice dealing with situations that the client typically finds difficult. An example of a behavioral assignment is shame-attacking exercises, in which clients are encouraged to do something ridiculous in public (e.g., yell in a public area; wear mismatched clothing items) to learn that nothing catastrophic happens.

One difficulty faced by REBT is the operationalization of what is an irrational thought. Haaga and Davison (1993) argue that the definition of what is rational involves ethics and values. They note that Ellis's ethics were that people should live long and happy lives and should maximize their individuality, freedom, self-interest, and self-control rather than submit to the control of others. Notably, these ethics are not consistent with collectivism values of many cultures, including Asian, Latino, and Arabic. Consequently, REBT may be less culturally sensitive than other forms of cognitive therapy.

Cognitive Therapy

Beck (1993) targets dysfunctional beliefs and faulty information processing through collaborative empiricism, in which client and therapist work together to identify and label errors in thinking, evaluate the evidence, and generate alternative, more realistic hypotheses. Typically, cognitive therapy begins with discussion of the role of thoughts in generating emotions. This includes discussion of how cognitive errors contribute to the misconstrual of situations. Such misconstrual is highlighted as the primary source of emotional distress. In addition, clients are helped to understand how misconstruals lead to behavioral choices that in turn compound the distress and confirm the misappraisals, contributing to a self-perpetuating cycle. The treatment rationale for targeting maladaptive thoughts per se as the problem flows naturally from this discussion.

Next, thoughts are recognized as being hypotheses rather than fact and are therefore open to questioning and challenge. This is the cognitive technique of distancing, or the ability to view one's thoughts more objectively and to draw a distinction between "I believe" and "I know." Detailed self-monitoring and downward arrowing of emotions and associated cognitions are instituted to identify specific beliefs, appraisals, and assumptions. Taking a personal scientist perspective enables individuals to become observers of their own cognitive biases and to be willing to consider alternatives to their own judgments. Once relevant cognitions are identified, they are categorized into types of errors, including dichotomous thinking, arbitrary inference, overgeneralization, and magnification, among others. The process of categorization, or labeling of thoughts, is consistent with a personal scientist model and facilitates an objective perspective by which the validity of the thoughts can be evaluated.

Therapists use Socratic questioning to help clients make guided discoveries and question their thoughts. If a client insists he cannot survive without his partner, the therapist may gently prod the client to ask himself whether he had survived before entering that partnership. This logical empiricism applies rational consideration to existing evidence, including ignored evidence, historical data, and alternative explanations for events. As an example, a therapist might ask a person who fears dying as a result of panic attacks to think about the number of times she has panicked and the result in each case.

Behavioral strategies include explicit activity schedules, graded tasks aimed at providing mastery and success, and behavioral experimentation, also called hypothesis testing. In behavioral experimentation, the client and therapist agree to test the validity of a particular thought through empirical data collection and experimentation. For the behavioral experiment to work, the behaviors, conditions, and negative thought being tested are clearly specified so that clients can fully test their hypotheses and evaluate whether they are confirmed by the data from the experiment. Review of the results is critical, especially to avoid emotion-based discounting of the results. For example, persons who judge that others will react negatively if asked for directions may be asked to test out their hypothesis by asking 10 different people for directions at a local shopping area. The evidence gathered from this experiment would be used to disconfirm blanket self-statements of being incapable of receiving helpful guidance from others. Clearly, the overlap with behavioral activation, problem solving, and exposure-based procedures is evident, although different mechanisms of action are implied within each strategy. In cognitive therapy, the behavioral steps are designed to collect data that challenge errors in thinking and generate more evidence-based thinking and to create new behaviors that help counteract previously held beliefs.

Throughout cognitive therapy, the therapist continuously models the skill of Socratic questioning, by asking questions or posing juxtapositions between an appraisal and the evidence. Affect-enhancing techniques, such as imagery (asking clients to imagine themselves facing a dreaded situation), are sometimes used for intensifying emotion, facilitating awareness of emotional responses that were previously out of awareness, accessing state-dependent core beliefs, restructuring cognitive–emotional networks, and modifying maladaptive emotional responses (Greenberg & Safran, 1989).

Another strategy is reverse role playing in which clients adopt the role of someone who possesses beliefs different from their own, while the therapist plays the role of someone with maladaptive beliefs; the client helps the therapist develop alternative beliefs. Sometimes modeling is employed before role playing, especially with children. Therapists overtly verbalize various appraisals of a situation and the client then imitates the therapist.

Based on the logical empiricism and data from behavioral experimentation, alternative, more evidence-based hypotheses are generated. As an example, the person who misappraises panic attacks as being physically dangerous may generate an alternative appraisal that panic attacks represent a definite change in physiology but one that is not harmful. Or the person who misappraises a frown as a sign of being ridiculed may generate a variety of alternative appraisals for a frown such as habit, fatigue, misunderstanding, concerns external to the conversation, or disagreement. In addition to surface level appraisals (e.g., "That person is frowning at me because I look foolish"), core level beliefs or schema (e.g., "I am not strong enough to withstand further distress" or "I am unlikable") are challenged and ultimately replaced with less dysfunctional schema.

The skills taught by the therapist are intended to be internalized by clients who learn to act as empiricists, collecting all available evidence to evaluate their judgments of a given situation. They learn the skill of Socratic questioning of their own reactions by using questions such as:

- What other plausible perspectives can I take about this matter?
- What factual evidence supports or refutes my beliefs?
- What are the pros and cons of continuing to see things the way I see them or of seeing things differently?
- What constructive action can I take to deal with my beliefs?
- What sincere advice would I give to a good friend with the same beliefs? (Newman, 2003)

Through practice, clients learn to be more deliberate and conscious of their own filtering mechanisms and compensate for them by appropriately considering aspects of their environment that may have been previously ignored.

Self-Instruction Training

Self-instruction training was developed by Meichenbaum (1977), who combined Ellis's model of irrational self-talk with knowledge of the developmental sequence through which children develop internal speech and verbal symbolic control over their behavior. In self-instruction training, internal dialogue is modified to include coping, task-oriented statements in the face of stressors. Four categories of self-statements are identified: preparing, confronting, coping, and reinforcing. Self-instruction training involves training clients to first become aware of emotional states produced by stressful situations so that those states become a cue for engaging in appropriate self-instruction. The client is then taught to become aware of maladaptive self-statements (e.g., "I can't deal with this"). Next, the therapist models appropriate behavior while verbalizing effective action strategies in each of the four categories. Specifically, these include an appraisal of task requirements (i.e., prepare), self-instructions that guide graded performance (i.e., confront), self-statements that stress personal adequacy and counteract worry (i.e., cope), and covert self-reinforcement for successful performance (i.e., reinforce). Then, the client performs the target behavior while verbalizing the self-instructions out loud, and then again while covertly rehearsing them. Therapist feedback assists in ensuring that constructive problem solving and self-talk replaces previous negative appraisals.

Indications and Contraindications
for Cognitive Strategies

Rational–emotive behavior therapy, cognitive therapy, and self-instruction training all are considered to be particularly useful for clients who have difficulty incorporating positive experiences into the way they think about themselves, their lives, and their futures. These strategies are also effective with individuals whose emotions and behaviors are based on faulty assumptions about themselves, their world, or their futures (Newman, 2003). Cognitive therapies should not be conducted in isolation from other behavioral strategies when maladaptive behaviors, cognitions, or emotions are maintained by maladaptive patterns of reinforcement (e.g., reinforcement from drug consumption) or when skill deficits (e.g., assertive skills) are apparent.

Cognitive strategies are closely aligned with the European/North American value of rational thinking. As noted by Hays and Imawasa (2006), emphasis on cognition, logic, verbal skills, and rational thinking can undercut the value of spirituality in many cultures. Related is the emphasis of cognitive strategies on reductionist cause-and-effect relations. In contrast, Asian cultural beliefs, for example, emphasize balance (or yin and yang), evaluation of systems holistically, and indirect causes for events. Thus, a client from a different culture may take into account additional causes for events that are not immediately obvious to a North American/ European therapist, thereby potentially undercutting the latter's attempts at cognitive restructuring. Another issue is locus of control, which tends to be more internal than external in Caucasians and more external than internal in many Asian cultures, wherein certain events are judged to be unrelated to one's own actions. Thus, what a therapist may judge to be a "logical outcome" may not coincide with the patient's beliefs. Cultural sensitivity of cognitive strategies mandates that therapists become knowledgeable about clients' cultural values and beliefs, something that would be achieved through functional analyses.

APPLICATIONS

To illustrate the versatility and range of CBT interventions, the applications of CBT for clients presenting with anxiety, depression, alcohol abuse, and bulimia nervosa are presented.

Anxiety Disorder

The first example is the application of CBT for an anxiety disorder, specifically panic disorder and agoraphobia (e.g., Craske & Barlow, 2008). Sarah had suffered from panic attacks for several years. She dreaded being on her own for fear of having a panic attack that would cause her to stop breathing and die. Consequently, she rarely left her home alone, and when she did, she would carry a number of "safety objects," such as antipanic medication and a list of phone numbers and locations of medical centers. A functional analysis was conducted of ways in which her cognitions about dying, her physical symptoms of shortness of breath and lightheadedness, and her behavior of avoiding being alone and reliance on safety objects contributed to each other and to the experience of panic and anxiety. In addition, Sarah was able to describe the contexts in which these cycles were most likely to develop, those being when her husband was traveling (when she became more afraid of being alone) and when she was fatigued (when Sarah became more concerned about shortness of breath). The treatment plan derived from this functional analysis. Treatment began with psychoeducation about the nature of fear and anxiety to correct Sarah's misconceptions about dying during panic attacks. In addition, she began to self-monitor her daily anxiety, panic attacks, and amount of time spent alone each day.

Next, Sarah was taught slow diaphragmatic breathing as a tool for helping her to cope with sensations of shortness of breath and anxiety in general and also as a tool for encouraging later exposure to feared situations and sensations. Cognitive restructuring was initiated, beginning with helping

Sarah to identify her appraisals about panic attacks, and in particular her thought that the sensations of shortness of breath and lightheadedness would intensify, reach the point of her no longer being able to breathe, and ultimately result in her death. Through Socratic questioning, Sarah was helped to regard her thoughts as hypotheses to be evaluated by her own evidence, which was that she had experienced those sensations on many occasions but had not died. However, her attempts to generate more evidence-based appraisals of those sensations were undercut by avoidance behaviors that prevented her from gathering information to disconfirm her fears of dying. That is, by avoiding being alone outside of home, Sarah did not have the chance to learn that she would not die of a panic attack. Thus, exposure therapy was initiated.

Exposure therapy targeted her fears of bodily sensations (i.e., shortness of breath and lightheadedness). For example, through repeated interoceptive exposure to breath holding exercises and hyperventilation, Sarah learned that sensations of shortness of breath and lightheadedness did not lead to harmful consequences and could be tolerated. The interoceptive exposure was conducted in session with therapist modeling and reinforcement and then practiced at home, first when her husband was present and then when alone. Similarly, through repeated in vivo exposure to progressively longer periods of time being alone and away from home, Sarah learned that the sensations were not life threatening even in situations in which she had most feared the panic attacks and even as she gradually let go of her safety signals (medications and lists of emergency contacts). Her in vivo exposure was extended to practices of leaving her home alone when she was fatigued, when her husband was out of town, and when she traveled to unfamiliar places where the locations of medical facilities was unknown. Also, interoceptive and in vivo exposure were combined, as Sarah practiced briefly holding her breath on her excursions of driving away from home. Relapse prevention involved encouragement for Sarah to continue her exposure practices, with consideration to high-risk situations in the future, such as when her husband traveled, and ways of using the breathing, cognitive, and exposure-based skills for managing them.

Depression

Daniel sought treatment for bouts of depressed mood, during which time it was difficult for him to complete his job and home responsibilities and his motivation and enjoyment of life were generally low. As described by Young, Rygh, Weinberger, and Beck (2008), CBT for depression began with a treatment rationale that emphasized the role of life events in limiting sources of positive reinforcement. For Daniel, the life event was the move he and his family made to a new city, which meant leaving his long-time friends and some loss of income in his new job. Areas of dysfunctional behavior were identified as limited physical exercise, lack of initiation of contact with coworkers, and lack of exploration of the new city. The therapist helped Daniel to become involved in more constructive activity by scheduling physical exercise and outings to different parts of the city. Problem-solving skills of identifying problems and generating solutions were used to design the outings. The exercise and outings served to increase sources of positive reinforcement since they were pleasant and mastery-related activities. Also, exercise was seen as a coping skill as it provided a source of distraction from negative affect, since by diverting attention through physical activity, cycles of depressed mood can be interrupted. In addition, the therapist helped Daniel to understand the way in which avoidance of contact with coworkers contributed to his lack of positive reinforcement and depressed mood. Thus, contacts with coworkers were scheduled, and were first behaviorally rehearsed through role play with the therapist in session.

Once some improvement had occurred in Daniel's behavioral functioning, attention shifted to the role of cognitions, all the while continuing the behavioral activities. The therapist helped Daniel to investigate the role of maladaptive schema, misappraisals of events, and unrealistic expectations, in the targeted problem area of friendships. Discussion of a specific event at work helped to elucidate Daniel's misappraisals. He reported that on one occasion his coworkers went to lunch as a group without him, which led to his appraisal that he would never fit in with this new group of people. He wondered why they should bother to get to know him anyway. Those appraisals in turn led to his behavior of sitting at his desk and eating lunch on his own, which served to confirm in his own mind the belief that he was boring and unlikable.

The therapist helped Daniel to identify errors in his thinking, such as overgeneralization from the single example of the coworkers having lunch without him, and selective abstraction of information, at the cost of other available information that he had gone to lunch with them on several other occasions. He was helped to generate alternative, more constructive appraisals, such as recognizing alternative attributions for why he was not asked to join the coworkers on that particular day. For example, Daniel realized that he was absent from his desk at the precise time that the coworkers were leaving the office for lunch, which may have explained why he was not asked to join them. In addition, Daniel was asked to provide examples of positive interactions with his coworkers as evidence that disconfirmed his belief of being boring and unlikable. These cognitive strategies were then combined with behavioral strategies of behavioral experimentation: specifically, Daniel would ask his coworkers to go to lunch with him (versus passively waiting for them to ask him) and initiate contact in various other ways. At this time, the behavioral strategies that were the emphasis of the initial phase of treatment were additionally used to gather data that disconfirmed Daniel's misappraisals. That is, his exercise and outings were discussed in terms of the disconfirmation they provided for his thoughts of being unable to fit into his new environment. With these skills, Daniel's depression lifted and his functioning improved.

Alcohol Abuse

David was a middle-aged husband and father who had developed a pattern of drinking to excess most evenings and most weekend days. His wife had threatened to leave him if he did not get his drinking under control. The outpatient CBT treatment for alcohol abuse/dependency (e.g., McCrady, 2008) began with motivational interviewing, in which the therapist, in an empathic manner, helped Daniel to understand the discordance between his substance use behaviors and his personal goals of health, self-esteem, and role responsibilities as a father and a husband. The therapist helped David to picture ways of achieving those desired goals, such as by exercising, and spending time with his family in the evenings and weekends rather than drinking, and generally encouraged David to mobilize his personal resources toward change. A decision for abstinence versus controlled drinking was made (abstinence usually is the preferred approach). Behavioral contracting was implemented so that each day without alcohol consumption, as well as engagement in physical exercise and family activities, was reinforced by a set of primary and secondary reinforcers. The latter included watching sports on television, favorite foods, and tokens that in accumulation were traded in for a new bicycle (cycling had been reinforcing for David in past years).

A full functional analysis of the feelings, thoughts, events, and behaviors preceding and following alcohol consumption was conducted, and the function of alcohol use was explored. In general, David used alcohol as a way of "letting go of stress" from his job and avoiding negative feelings about himself. Alcohol use was prompted by the belief that it would make him feel better. In addition, difficulties communicating with his wife with whom he had frequent arguments led him to use alcohol as a way of "escape" in the home environment. David was taught sobriety strategies of stimulus control (which meant to remove all alcohol from his home), and use of imagery (e.g., "surfing with the urge" or "attacking the urge") to survive urges, and learn by observation that urges do subside. His cognitive distortions about alcohol were also addressed, particularly his overly positive expectancies about alcohol, by pairing the perceived positive consequences with the real negative consequences (e.g., more arguments with wife, poor health). In addition, behavioral alternatives to alcohol consumption were selected, to not only fill the gap in time and effort that used to be involved in alcohol consumption, but also to provide alternative sources of positive reinforcement. These included physical exercise and activities with his family, already behaviorally contracted.

Next, skills training was implemented for skill deficits in managing work-related stress. These included relaxation training, cognitive restructuring regarding misappraisals of events at work that generated unnecessary stress (e.g., beliefs that he would be heavily criticized for his work), and problem solving (e.g., ways of dealing with a coworker whose mistakes impacted performance evaluations of David's work). In addition, David was encouraged to enter couples communication training with his wife. Furthermore, the therapist helped David to cope with substance availability cues, by controlled exposure to alcohol cues in the safety of the treatment setting. This was done to extinguish craving responses. Thus, the therapist brought alcohol to the session, so that the smell and sight of the alcohol could serve as a CS to be extinguished by not being consumed. At the same time, David was taught skills for managing exposure to alcohol in daily life, which meant learning to disassociate from environments outside of the home previously associated with alcohol consumption, combined with assertiveness training in how to refuse peer pressure to reestablish drinking. This was achieved through role playing with the therapist. With these skills, Daniel was able to achieve control over his drinking with only occasional lapses.

Bulimia Nervosa

Jenny was a 23-year-old, single female. For the past 6 years, she had developed a pattern of binging on food, followed by purging in the form of vomiting and laxatives, and a subsequent period of relative dietary restriction. The binge/purge cycle occurred approximately two times per week. CBT for bulimia nervosa, as outlined by Fairburn, Cooper, Shafran, and Wilson (2008), involves four stages. In the first stage, the aims are to engage clients in treatment, something that can be particularly difficult for eating disorders when there is ambivalence about treatment goals. Jenny was ambivalent but was also worried about the effects on her health and future relationships and thus was self-motivated for learning ways of changing her binge/purge behavior. Through the help of the therapist, Jenny established her own functional analysis: depressed mood and not having anyone to "do things with" served as triggers to her binge eating; overvaluation of shape and weight and their control contributed to her binging and purging; and dieting and compensatory vomiting and laxative misuse encouraged binging in the future. The treatment rationale naturally flowed from this analysis. Self-monitoring was also initiated in the first stage, starting with monitoring of eating habits. Weekly in-session weighing was established, along with instructions to not weigh herself at any other times, thereby putting a limit on her excessive body checking. She was also educated about the natural fluctuations that occur in daily weight and myths about eating and weight. Jenny was then given a regular eating schedule of three meals plus two snacks per day, combined with instructions to prevent herself from vomiting and using laxatives (i.e., response prevention). To deal with the urges to eat at times other than the specified meals and snacks, Jenny was encouraged to engage in competing activities, such as socializing or going for a walk, and to observe the urge to eat to learn that it is temporary and does pass.

The first stage of CBT was spread out over eight sessions across 4 weeks. The second stage of treatment involved a joint review of progress and continuation of the plan from the first stage with some minor revisions. For example, Jenny had tried to deal with her urges by reading magazines, but they included advertisements for food that only increased her urges to eat at times when it was not appropriate to eat. Thus, alternative ways of dealing with the urges were established (i.e., puzzle games). The third stage of CBT addressed Jenny's overevaluation of shape and weight, which in itself comprised several steps. She was helped to build a pie chart with the slices representing aspects of life that were important to her. Jenny's biggest slice, or the slice that was most important to her, was shape, weight, and eating. The therapist then reviewed the consequences of overevaluating shape and weight, including the fact that Jenny dieted, thought too much about food and eating, engaged in excessive body checking, and thought too much about shape and weight and feeling "fat." Next, Jenny was asked to schedule valued activities that matched other aspects of her life to increase their value. This meant scheduling activities for returning to college to complete her bachelor's degree, as well as joining clubs to meet new people. In addition, Jenny's feelings of fatness were addressed by teaching her to recognize the trigger to such feelings, which was depressed mood. Problem solving was then employed for dealing with negative mood states as an alternative to overeating to cope with negative mood.

Also, the therapist helped Jenny realize the ways in which dietary restraint contributed to her overevaluation of weight and shape. This led to dealing directly with the dietary restraint. In particular, rules associated with dietary restraint were broken, because such rules promote a continued cycle of dietary restriction and binging. For example, foods that Jenny had been avoiding for fear of loss of control or weight gain (e.g., breads, pasta, chocolate) were gradually reintroduced.

The fourth and final stage of CBT focused on maintaining the changes in treatment and minimizing relapse. The latter was achieved by educating Jenny about the risk of relapse, the importance of early detection of problem behaviors, and ways of managing those behaviors based on the principles learned in treatment.

LONGER CASE WITH A DIVERSE CLIENTELE

Maria is a 29-year-old female who presented with severe social anxiety and major depression. Maria sought treatment as a result of threat of job loss due to her avoidance of fellow coworkers and resultant difficulties in completing her assigned work tasks in a timely and competent manner. Maria was born in North America, but her parents, with whom she lived, were first-generation immigrants from Mexico. Their fluency in English language was limited. Maria's young brother lived with his wife and children in the same neighborhood, as did several members of the extended family. Maria was close with her family and their collective goals.

In terms of presenting symptoms, Maria reported difficulty in initiating and maintaining conversations, asking for help, saying "no" to unreasonable requests, entering a room full of people, disclosing information about herself, asking questions in meetings, and public speaking. She experienced these difficulties mostly at work and in any unfamiliar social situation. However, in the context of her family and family friends, Maria was able to interact appropriately and receive enjoyment from interactions. Maria also had symptoms of depression, including sadness, lack of energy, oversleeping, and feelings of hopelessness about the future. She occasionally had thoughts of suicide, but these were fleeting thoughts and she did not endorse full suicidal ideation.

The pattern of social anxiety was apparent in childhood. She had few friends in elementary school. She recalled specific instances during childhood when she felt particularly humiliated, such as when her classmates laughed at her when she tripped on the playground at school and when she mispronounced words (teasing occurred mostly from non-Latino students in her culturally diverse elementary school). In addition, her social anxiety was magnified by a salient birthmark across her left cheek. During childhood, she recalled instances of other kids staring at her and making comments about her birthmark. Her social anxiety at school was further fueled by language barriers between school and home. As her parents spoke little English, they were seldom able to help their children with homework. Maria felt too anxious to ask teachers for help, and consequently, she underachieved. During high school, Maria developed a few acquaintance-type friendships, but never to the degree of close confidantes. She remained on the periphery of social situations and continued to be very self-conscious about her birthmark. She generally avoided social situations outside of those involving her extended family. Even though her parents were concerned that Maria was not and never had been involved in a romantic relationship, they were reassured by her closeness with the family.

After graduating high school, Maria attended local college. She found little enjoyment in college and continued to have difficulty making friends. Also, she struggled with grades and exams, especially given the limits imposed by her avoidance of professors and teaching assistants. Thus, she dropped out of college after the first year and began a clerical position in a medical records department of a local hospital. Her performance reviews have been up and down; most recently, her boss informed Maria that unless she learned to interact with her fellow coworkers and get her work done on time, her job was in jeopardy. At this point, and with the encouragement of her family, Maria sought help first from her priest, who in turn recommended a resource for mental health treatment in the community.

The initial diagnostic assessment indicated a generalized type of social anxiety disorder and major depression. In terms of the functional analysis, it was apparent that there were many social situations that triggered her anxiety, which she avoided whenever possible. When in those social situations, Maria was particularly reactive to any verbal or nonverbal signal that could be interpreted as either ridicule or disgust at her appearance. It also become apparent that Maria possessed a basic behavioral repertoire of social skills, as evident in her interactions with her family and family friends. However, anxiety interfered with appropriate social skills outside of those family-type situations. Also, she lacked the skills of assertive communication in general. In terms of her cognitive appraisals, Maria believed that others ridiculed her and/or did not find her to be interesting. Also, she felt very self-conscious about the birthmark on her face which she believed led others to judge her as ugly and disgusting. Her core belief was that no one would ever like her, something that was "confirmed" by the absence of close friendships or romantic relationships. In terms of her physiological responses, she experienced sweating, racing heart, and shortness of breath as she anticipated and entered social situations at work or in unfamiliar settings. In turn, she interpreted these physical symptoms as being obvious to others and another source of their criticism of her. In terms of behaviors, in addition to the overt avoidance and refusal to enter and participate in a wide array of social situations outside of the family context, Maria also had a number of more subtle patterns of avoidance. She rarely looked at people directly in the eye, and she turned her face so that the birthmark was less apparent to those with whom she was interacting. These avoidance behaviors were reinforced negatively by the reduction in acute anxiety they produced. In addition, avoidance of unfamiliar social situations was further reinforced by the positive family reinforcement for remaining "close to home." Also, the overt and more subtle avoidance behaviors served to confirm her negative expectations for how others viewed her, which contributed to further avoidance behavior. Furthermore, her avoidant behaviors and negative cognitions contributed to her depressed mood, which in turn contributed to low motivation to deal with social situations. Finally, her withdrawn style of staying on the periphery of social situations and failing to establish eye contact was uncomfortable for those around her, to the point that her coworkers had stopped making efforts to engage in conversation with Maria. She interpreted their behavior as evidence for their dislike of her.

After conducting the functional analysis through interviewing and assessment by self-report questionnaires in the first session, the therapist used Maria's behaviors in the second session as an opportunity to review the functional analysis and provide a treatment rationale.

Therapist: I notice that you are sitting with the side of your face that does not have the birthmark toward me. Does it make you more comfortable to sit that way?

Maria: Yes, that way you don't have to look at my birthmark.

Therapist: What do you think would happen if I saw your birthmark?

Maria: I don't know. . . . I think it would make you uncomfortable and disgusted.

Therapist: So, let's think about this in terms of the ways in which thoughts, behaviors, and feelings influence each other. The thought that I would be disgusted leads to your behavior of positioning yourself so that I don't see the birthmark, and that makes you feel less anxious.

Maria: Yes, it's all I can do.

Therapist: I can see how that would help you in the moment. I am wondering, though, what the long term effects might be.

Maria: I am not sure what you mean.

Therapist: Right now you have a thought that others are disgusted and so you turn away. If you did not turn away…if you showed your birthmark openly…you could learn whether people actually are disgusted or not.

Maria: But I can remember how horrible it felt when other kids made fun of my birthmark.

Therapist: That must have been very upsetting for you as a kid. I guess the question is whether the way some kids treated you back then is a good indicator of how others would treat you now. By turning your face away, you never get to learn how others will actually react or how to cope with their reactions.

Following a treatment rationale that emphasized skills for developing less negative, harmful thinking and replacing avoidant behaviors with approach behaviors, therapy began by learning to self-monitor occasions when Maria became anxious in anticipation of or entering a social situation. The focus was on specific appraisals she was making and the particular cues within social situations that triggered further anxiety (e.g., particular facial expressions and silences in conversations). Her avoidant behaviors were monitored as well, with close attention to not only overt avoidance, but more subtle forms of avoidance, specifically those surrounding her attempts to hide her birthmark. Maria was encouraged to gather this information as a way of becoming a personal scientist. In addition, a hierarchy of social situations was developed that would be the target of practice throughout treatment. Emphasis was given to situations in the work context, given the pressure from her boss to improve her skills at work or else lose her job. In addition, the therapist and Maria jointly decided to achieve mastery in the workplace before working on unfamiliar social situations, when the role of family reinforcement patterns would be additionally addressed.

Next, Maria was taught slow diaphragmatic breathing as a tool for helping her to deal with her anxiety in social situations. She first practiced this exercise at home alone and then practiced in more distracting environments, such as when driving. Next, she used the breathing exercise every time she responded to a phone call at work and when she was approached by fellow coworkers. The final step was to incorporate the breathing exercise in her deliberate exposure practices to situations listed on her hierarchy.

Cognitive restructuring was initiated with a discussion of the types of errors that are typical to anxious thinking; overestimating the likelihood of negative events and catastrophizing the meaning of negative events. Maria was encouraged to use her self-monitoring to identify examples of each type of error, and the therapist began teaching the skill of using evidence to replace distorted thinking with more evidence-based thinking.

Therapist: So, on your monitoring form, you recorded that when you walked into the coffee room at work, everyone noticed that you were sweating and thought that you were disgusting. What led you to believe that?

Maria: Well, just that I felt so uncomfortable, so I was sure they would notice me and judge me.

Therapist: So your feelings were telling you that? What actually happened in the situation?

Maria: Nothing really. Someone offered me a coffee cup and I poured myself some coffee and stood at the counter for a few minutes, just listening quietly to the conversation.

Therapist: So, was there any action taken on the part of the others to indicate that they were disgusted by you?

Maria: No, they just kept talking.

Therapist: So what does that tell you about your thought?

Maria: Maybe I was jumping to a conclusion—maybe I just assumed they were disgusted and I didn't think of other possibilities.

Therapist: So, what would be a different way of thinking in this situation?

Maria: I mean, it's hard for me to believe, but I suppose maybe they didn't really care that I was sweating, or maybe they didn't even notice at all.

The goal was to balance thinking away from always expecting rejection and ridicule and toward the notion that social rejection and ridicule were probably less likely than what Maria was anticipating. As recommended by Organista (2006), in his discussions of the modification of cognitive therapy for Hispanic/Latino clients, this was achieved by encouraging Maria to switch from "half truths" in her thinking into "whole truths," or to always follow a negative appraisal with another appraisal that represents the "other side of the coin." Another goal was to encourage Maria to cope with momentary negative social interactions so that they became less catastrophic than she judged them to be. The therapist engaged in logical discussion of how others interpret momentary social negativity or awkwardness to help Maria generate alternative points of view.

Therapist: Let's think of all the possible ways that someone else might judge a moment of silence in a conversation.

Maria: All that comes to mind is that they feel awkward and they get angry at me for making them feel that way.

Therapist: Okay, so that is a possibility, but what else might they think? Think of all the times that people have pauses in their own conversations. How might they think about that?

Maria: Well, maybe that it was awkward but they wouldn't get angry.

Therapist: Yes, what else?

Maria: Maybe it happens so often that it doesn't even phase them.

Therapist: Another good possibility. What else?

Maria: Maybe they blame themselves and not the other person.

Therapist: So you can see there are a number of ways of interpreting the same situation. Which one is most helpful to you?

The issue that next arose was Maria's concern of "what if someone is disgusted?" The therapist helped Maria to face that possibility and develop ways of coping. The therapist role-played with Maria how to respond behaviorally if someone showed signs of disgust and how to generate different possibilities about what it would mean if others were to show disgust.

Therapist: So, let's face the worst for a moment and imagine that you are out in public and someone looks at your birthmark and then shows a visual grimace of disgust. Let's consider how you would cope with that situation.

Maria: I would feel just horrible and would want to hide away as quickly as possible.

Therapist: That is one way of coping, but as we have talked about before, what is the end result of the hiding away?

Maria: I just become more and more afraid.

Therapist: What is another way of coping? What could you say or do in that situation?

Maria: Well, I could look at someone else instead of at the person who is clearly upset by my appearance.

Therapist: Yes, what else?

Maria: I could tell them to stop staring at me.

Therapist: You could. What else?

Maria: I could tell myself that person was mean and not everyone reacts the same way as he did.

Therapist: Good, so you see there are a number of ways of coping, even in a difficult situation.

At this point, Maria broke into tears. She described an instance in elementary school when she found a group of kids laughing at words written on the bathroom wall; later she went back to look at the words. They were about her, referring to her as ugly and deformed. The therapist encouraged Maria to describe the entire situation, from beginning to end, and her thoughts, feelings, and behaviors. By so doing, the therapist shifted to an exposure-based model of helping Maria to habituate to the memory of the trauma, all the while providing support and validation for Maria's distress. Over the next week, Maria was asked to write about the traumatic experience each day, to continue to habituate to the memory of the event. This was very helpful for Maria, and it made it much easier for her to continue treatment.

Extensive role playing and behavioral rehearsal were next conducted to facilitate response generalization of Maria's verbal and nonverbal skills of socializing to work-related situations. The situations listed in her hierarchy included asking questions of a coworker, giving compliments, asking a question for purposes of clarification in a meeting, asking coworkers for help, and asking her boss a question. Role plays and behavioral rehearsal shaped her behaviors, with the use of therapist reinforcement and feedback. These were difficult at first, but with continued practice and feedback, Maria became more comfortable. Practice included coping with a variety of responses (i.e., coping with negative responses and positive responses from others). Also, multiple behaviors were rehearsed in relation to each situation listed on her hierarchy, including direct eye contact and not hiding her birthmark. In the end, the goal was for Maria to be able to look people directly in the eye with the birthmark clearly visible on her face. She and her therapist agreed that only by so doing would Maria be able to develop more adaptive appraisals and realize that others were less likely to show disgust than she anticipated, and that there would be ways in which she could effectively manage discomfort or awkwardness on occasions when others did stare or show a negative response to her birthmark. Every in-session role play was followed by a homework assignment of practice in which Maria was to complete the social interaction as often as possible, with the use of breathing retraining and cognitive skills to help her cope with anxiety.

After several weeks, it became apparent that Maria's depressive symptoms of lack of motivation and fatigue interfered with completion of homework assignments. This barrier was identified and addressed in terms of a functional analysis, which helped Maria to recognize that avoidance, even if motivated by depression and low motivation, contributed to negative beliefs about herself and the way she thought others would react to her. The self-efficacy and motivating effects that would come from behavioral activation were discussed and activities that were positively reinforcing were identified. Maria had an interest in painting, and even though she had her own materials, she had not painted for some time. Thus, she contracted to engage in painting at least twice a week on her own. Contracting of times when to paint was done with care to avoid conflict with her family responsibilities. Next, a problem-solving approach was used to address the issue of fatigue by considering times of day when she was most able to complete her exposure assignments. Up until this point, Maria had tended to procrastinate and leave her exposure practices until the end of the day (as a form of avoidance), which coincided with the time at which she was most fatigued. Thus, she was encouraged to complete the assignments (i.e., asking a coworker for help or clarification) early in the day.

Another impediment was Maria's tendency to discount her accomplishments. After exposure therapy practices, instead of appraising what had been learned in a constructive manner, she was inclined to think that others were simply being positive toward her because they felt pity toward her.

Therapist: So, how did the practice go this week?

Maria: Well, I asked my coworker about his drive to work this morning and the traffic, and it ended up developing into a conversation that lasted for over 10 minutes.

Therapist: That's great. Well done!"

Maria: I don't know.... I think he just felt sorry for me so he kept talking.

Therapist: Okay, so that is one way of interpreting his behavior. Using our cognitive skills, can you think of other reasons for his behavior?

Maria: It's hard for me to believe that he really wanted to speak with me, but maybe he did.

Therapist: Were there positive aspects to the conversation?

Maria: I smiled, I looked at him as he spoke, and he laughed.

Therapist: So, what does that tell you?

Maria: Well, maybe it was okay after all. I have to realize that people are not as negative about me as I think.

Therapist: That's right, and continued practice in social situations will help you to develop that realization.

About midway through the treatment, Maria's assignment was to ask a fellow coworker to help her on a particular work project. The response that Maria received was judged by her to be dismissive. Maria felt like a fool for asking and was concerned that the coworker was disgusted by her appearance. She became depressed and dejected by this experience. The therapist focused on the role of interpretations about the apparent dismissal as well as the importance of coping with occasional social rejections as a part of normal social interaction. Again, behavioral rehearsal and role playing were used to practice different ways of coping, cognitively and behaviorally, with negative social interactions. Furthermore, Maria was encouraged to continue to ask her coworkers for help as was appropriate to the task at hand, so she could gather more evidence about the likelihood of rejection and ways of coping with negative responses from others. These new experiences tended to be more positive and offset the earlier negative one.

Once some mastery was developed in social situations at work, Maria and her therapist agreed that it was time to address unfamiliar social situations, such as joining a painting or exercise class. Relevant to designing these practices was the issue of family reinforcement for her closeness with the family, and their expectation that Maria should attend every extended family function and always be accompanied by a family member on outings. Although anxiety provoking, Maria realized the importance of learning to cope with social situations outside of her family. She was encouraged to use assertiveness to explain to her family the importance of some independence from them, especially as it would increase her chances of dating, something that her parents were most eager for her to do. She and therapist role-played ways of communicating assertively with her parents in a way that was respectful. For example, an assertive request to spend time shopping on her own was prefaced by statements such as "with all due respect, mama, I need to learn how to be on my own." Also, her brother was quite supportive of Maria's attempts in this regard and helped Maria to practice ways of communicating with their parents in a respectful manner.

After 20 weeks of treatment, Maria had begun to achieve some mastery of interacting with her coworkers, and she was beginning to work on unfamiliar social situations. She felt as if she was learning a set of skills for how to interact in social situations and was becoming less self-conscious about her birthmark. When she entered a social situation, her first thought remained that others would find her ugly or boring, but she was gradually gaining behavioral evidence to counteract those beliefs. Some of her coworkers had reciprocated and she was now joining them at lunch. In addition, as part of her hierarchy, Maria had arranged to meet with her boss on a biweekly basis to check on her progress from his point of view. This had proved helpful as he was generally supportive of her improved interactional skills. Furthermore, Maria had joined a painting class, where she had initiated conversations with another student in the painting class and was looking forward to further contact with that person both inside and outside of the class. Her depression had lifted and she was feeling more hopeful about the future. With her brother's help, her parents were responding well to her requests to do things on her own, away from the family, especially as these activities did not detract from Maria's enjoyment of family activities. Maria still had a number of situations to practice, but she had made good progress and was motivated to continue.

OBSTACLES OR PROBLEMS USING THIS APPROACH

As elucidated by Young (1990), the success of CBT depends on a number of factors: clients having ready access to their feelings and thoughts and identifiable target problems; being quickly able to develop collaborative relationships with the therapist without the therapist–client relationship itself needing to be a major focus of treatment; and thoughts, feelings, and behaviors that can be modified through empirical analysis, logical discourse, experimentation, and behavioral practice (Young, 1990). Thus, barriers to any of these factors are likely to become obstacles to successful implementation of CBT.

As is likely the case with every psychotherapy, the evidence indicates that the more severe and complex the presentation at treatment entry, the poorer than usual the response to CBT (e.g., Haby, Donnelly, Corry, & Vos, 2006). Medical comorbidity (e.g., Iosifescu et al., 2003) and life stressors (Sanderson & Bruce, 2007), including poor marital relations (e.g., Dewey & Hunsley, 1990), also are associated with poorer outcomes from CBT.

Another type of complexity is comorbid personality disorders, which tend to lessen or slow the response to CBT for anxiety and depression (e.g., McCabe & Antony, 2005; Robins & Hayes, 1993). In this literature, poorer outcomes do *not* mean nonresponse, but rather less improvement than otherwise occurs. The following section considers possible explanations for the negative effects of initial severity and complexity upon outcomes, and potential remedies.

One pathway through which severity and complexity may negatively impact CBT is by decreasing the personal resources available for the effort involved in this form of therapy. In other words, learning new ways of thinking and behaving takes effort. Learning new appraisal strategies is difficult, even for the person who is not dealing with a psychological disorder, since we all have a tendency to selectively attend to stimuli and information that support our beliefs and ignore or discount contrary information. Under conditions of elevated distress, these tendencies to be selective become even stronger. That is, we are all more likely to rely on cognitive "shortcuts" under times of stress; distorted patterns of thinking are such shortcuts. Alternative modes of information processing that require greater resource expenditure, such as attending to data rather than to prior expectancies, are obstructed by high levels of stress (e.g., Ford & Kruglanski, 1995). Learning to behave and think in a different way and face challenging situations takes even more effort. And yet, this type of resource expenditure is exactly what is demanded by CBT. Hence, excessively high levels of distress and stress may impede engagement in the processes of CBT, thus possibly explaining why initial severity and complexity, medical comorbidity, life stressors, and personality disorders are associated with a lesser or slower response to CBT.

Limitations to personal resources may be addressed by slowing the pace of CBT. Also, reminders of coping skills can be incorporated, such as written prompts (on cards) for how to generate evidence-based thoughts. Workbooks are another resource that can serve as a continuous reminder of cognitive and behavioral strategies. Greater structure to homework practices and reinforcement for accomplishment of those practices may be helpful. Also, significant others and community supports can be "recruited" to give encouragement for cognitive and behavioral skills practices in the home environment. For particularly high levels of physiological stress, relaxation techniques may be a useful start to each session, to facilitate attention and learning in the remainder of the session. Furthermore, problem-solving approaches may be applied to deal with ongoing life stressors.

Another explanation for why initial severity and complexity predicts poorer than usual response to CBT is that attempts to manage one specific area of cognitive and behavioral dysfunction are thwarted by other areas of dysfunction. Attempts to deal with an anxiety disorder, for example, may be interrupted by dysregulation of interpersonal processes in the client who additionally suffers from a personality disorder. CBT most often is very focused in its application, targeting specific problem areas. The focused nature of CBT may render it less effective with more complex presentations than more broadly focused approaches, although, this remains an empirical question. Unified CBT approaches that have relevance to a broad array of negative emotions, cognitions, and behaviors are a potential option (Allen, McHugh, & Barlow, 2008).[3] Another option is to provide more than one focused CBT at the same time, such as simultaneous delivery of CBT specifically focused on anxiety and CBT specifically focused on depression. However, preliminary evidence suggests that such dual focus may eventually detract from the overall benefits of CBT (Craske et al., 2007). Alternatively, CBT may be combined with psychotropic medications for complex and severe presentations, although such combination treatments are not without their own difficulties, which are discussed in later section.

Thirdly, initial severity and complexity may lower motivation to engage in any or all aspects of CBT, including homework. Engagement includes being part of the case formulation, learning the behavioral and cognitive strategies, and most importantly, putting them into practice. As noted earlier, homework practice is a significant mediator of treatment outcome, and low motivation is likely to lessen homework compliance and therefore

---

[3] Unified CBT protocols are yet to be fully tested in comparison to specifically targeted CBT protocols.

eventual success of CBT. Motivation is likely to be influenced by a myriad of factors, including those inherent to the problem that is the target for treatment. For example, low motivation and low self-efficacy that is characteristic of depressed mood are likely to lessen motivation to engage in CBT. Similarly, ambivalence about change in relation to drug use, anorexia, and other disorders is likely to decrease the motivation to engage in CBT, as will competing sources of reinforcement for maladaptive behaviors. For example, parents who give attention to distress and fail to give attention to nondistressed behaviors in children with separation anxiety disorder may inadvertently reinforce the separation anxiety and thereby interfere with engagement in CBT. Similarly, significant others who take on the daily home responsibilities and chores that are no longer being completed by their overly anxious partners may inadvertently reinforce the latter's anxiety and thereby reduce motivation for CBT.

Motivational interviewing (Miller & Rollnick, 1991) may be warranted in cases of ambivalence, and behavioral contracting may be used to provide extrinsic reinforcement for engagement in CBT. In addition, when significant others are providing reinforcement that is counter to the goals of CBT, they can be included in the treatment. This can be especially valuable with CBT for children, where a large part of the treatment involves parent training to maximize parental reinforcement of adaptive childhood behaviors relative to maladaptive behaviors (e.g., Barrett, Farrell, Dadds, & Boulter, 2005). Involving significant others in every aspect of treatment, including attention to the reinforcement patterns for anxious versus nonanxious behaviors, also improves the effects of CBT for adult anxiety (e.g., Cerny, Barlow, Craske, & Himadi, 1987).

Other factors likely to influence motivation include general beliefs about etiology and/or treatment process that run counter to CBT theories and principles. Degree of belief in the rationale for CBT is linked to more rapid and overall better treatment outcomes (e.g., Addis & Jacobson, 2000). For example, beliefs that "unconscious conflicts" are responsible for a presenting problem may impede motivation to engage in CBT. Education about the role of conscious cognitions and behaviors may increase the motivation to engage in CBT, particularly if combined with relevant examples from the individual's own experience.

The issue of conflicting beliefs sometimes arises when CBT is combined with psychotropic medications. Clearly, CBT is aimed at teaching self-control skills for changing maladaptive cognitions and behaviors. Psychotropic medications likely foster the belief that problems are due to neurochemical imbalances, which in turn may lessen the perceived importance of CBT as a treatment. In accord, patients with "free floating" anxiety who received EMG biofeedback without the aid of medication practiced relaxation exercises more frequently than those who additionally received diazepam (Lavallee, Lamontagne, Pinard, Annable, & Tetreault, 1977). Other evidence indicates that attribution of therapeutic gains to medications rather than personal mastery may contribute to the occasions when the combination of CBT with medications is inferior to CBT alone. That is attribution of therapeutic gains to an anti-anxiety medication in patients who were treated with the drug in combination with either exposure or relaxation training predicted subsequent withdrawal symptoms and relapse (Basoglu et al., 1994). These attribution effects can potentially be offset by initiating CBT as a first-line treatment before medication and by adding CBT booster sessions following the termination of medication. By so doing, improvements would be more likely to be attributed to CBT, thereby encouraging motivation to engage in CBT, and reducing relapse when medication is withdrawn.

Finally, there may be cultural barriers to CBT. As indicated throughout this text, a proper functional analysis takes into account cultural factors that influence problem behaviors, emotions, or thoughts. Moreover, cultural contexts and constraints are considered when designing and implementing CBT. This form of therapy is heavily aligned with European and North American values of change, open self-disclosure, independence and autonomy, and rational thinking (see Hays & Iwamasa, 2006). Such values often are at odds with values of harmony, family, and spirituality that are deeply embedded in Asian, Latino, Arabic, African American, and other cultures. Thus, culturally responsive CBT recognizes these influences and modifies the strategies accordingly. As indicated in the next chapter, the evidence suggests that such modifications are effective.

5

Evaluation

Cognitive–behavioral therapy (CBT) is the most empirically supported psychotherapy. Meta-analyses of the effectiveness of CBT usually combine therapies that are mostly cognitive therapy in nature with ones that are more cognitive–behavioral in nature. A review of 16 meta-analyses evaluated CBT across a wide range of disorders (Butler, Chapman, Forman, & Beck, 2006). The disorders were as follows: adult unipolar depression, adolescent unipolar depression, generalized anxiety disorder, panic disorder with and without agoraphobia, social phobia, obsessive–compulsive disorder, posttraumatic stress disorder, schizophrenia, marital distress, anger, bulimia nervosa, internalizing childhood disorders, sexual offending, and chronic pain. Comparisons were usually with no treatment or with nondirective supportive counseling as a placebo control. Very few studies have compared CBT to other active psychotherapies, such as psychodynamic therapies. The results of the review were as follows.

First, CBT was considered highly effective for adult unipolar depression, generalized anxiety disorder, panic disorder with or without agoraphobia, social phobia, posttraumatic stress disorder, and childhood anxiety and depressive disorders, with a large mean effect size of .95 (SD =.08) in comparison to no-treatment, wait list, or placebo controls. These effects are consistent with a recent meta-analysis of CBT for anxiety disorders, excluding specific phobias, by Norton and Price (2007); CBT was more effective than no-treatment or attention placebo conditions across all disorders. Interestingly, the frequency and duration of sessions, and the format of individual versus group treatment, were not related to outcomes (Norton & Price, 2007).

Butler and colleagues (2006) further concluded that CBT was highly effective for bulimia nervosa (mean effect size = 1.27, SD = .11) and more so than pharmacotherapy. Also, CBT added to the pharmacotherapy treatment of schizophrenia. Moderate effect sizes were obtained from CBT for marital distress, anger, childhood somatic disorders, and several chronic pain conditions, relative to control groups (mean effect size = .62, SD = .11), whereas the efficacy of CBT for sexual offending was relatively low (effect size = .35).

Results from CBT for anxiety and depression appear to be somewhat less effective in late life samples relative to middle age or childhood/adolescent samples (e.g., Kraus, Kunik, & Stanley, 2007). However, CBT is still more effective than treatment as usual for late life depression (Laidlaw et al., 2008), and a meta-analysis indicated that CBT was more effective than wait list and active control conditions in the treatment of late life anxiety disorders (Hendriks, Oude Voshaar, Keijsers, Hoogduin, & van Balkom, 2008).

Generally, the results from CBT tend to maintain over follow-up intervals that extend from 6 to 24 months (e.g., Butler et al., 2006; Haby et al., 2006; Norton & Price, 2007). Butler and colleagues concluded that there was evidence for maintenance of treatment gains for depression, generalized anxiety disorder, panic disorder, social phobia, obsessive compulsive disorder, sexual offending, schizophrenia, and childhood internalizing disorders. The long-term effects were particularly robust for depression and panic disorder, where the rate of relapse was almost half of the rate of relapse that follows from pharmacotherapy.

However, some relapse and nonresponse does occur. Most of the research on this topic pertains to CBT for depression. In a meta-analysis of research studies specifically focused on relapse following CBT for depression, 29% relapsed within 1 year and 54% within 2 years of discontinuing CBT (Vittengl, Clark, Dunn, & Jarrett, 2007). Notably, these rates are lower than rates of relapse following discontinuation of pharmacotherapy, and continuation of CBT decreased relapse in comparison to other continuation treatments. Dobson and colleagues (2008) replicated these effects, with less relapse upon discontinuation of cognitive therapy relative to pharmacotherapy. Patterns of relapse have been much less well studied in the context of other disorders. In terms of anxiety disorders, one study reported that 27% of panic disorder individuals who had reached a panic-free status by the end of CBT received additional treatment for panic over the next 24 months (Brown & Barlow, 1995). Clearly, there is need for much more research on patterns of relapse, treatment seeking following CBT, and ways for offsetting relapse. In the area of depression treatment, for example, mindfulness-based techniques have been shown to reduce relapse (Teasdale et al., 2002). The role of mindfulness in the context of relapse for other disorders remains to be investigated.

In nonresearch settings, reports regarding relapse and nonresponse, albeit few in number, are less promising than in research settings. Specifically, one review of naturalistic studies found that short-term CBT for a variety of disorders had limited long-term benefits, 2 to 14 years after treatment was delivered (Durham et al., 2005). For example, in the studies of anxiety disorders, 64% of participants reported receiving interim treatment for anxiety over the follow-up interval. It remains to be seen whether the results obtained in real-world settings are less impressive than in research trials because of the nature of the patient population (possibly being more severe or complex than patients who enter research trials) and/or because CBT is not delivered with as much competency or focus as in controlled efficacy trials. Reviews of the child literature have identified core differences in the delivery of community-based versus research-based interventions. These differences include a broad, multi-problem focus and flexibility in responding to issues that clients bring to each session (in an effort to treat the "whole" client) in the former case compared to a clearly delineated narrow focus and imposing of an agenda and a preplanned structured manual in the latter case (e.g., Weisz, Jensen, & McLeod, 2005). These core differences may account for the substantially lower rates of effectiveness in community-based settings compared to research studies, at least for childhood disorders.

Another caveat to the success of CBT is the percentage of individuals who either refuse to enter therapy or who drop out after starting CBT. It is hard to estimate the numbers who refuse to begin CBT, although Issakidis and Andrews (2004) reported that 30.4% of a sample of 731 individuals attending an anxiety disorders clinic did not start treatment. Also, pretreatment attrition was associated with higher levels of depression. Rates of entry into CBT may be improved by preparatory information, such as pamphlets or videos that depict CBT methods, something particularly valuable for minority groups (Organista, 2006). More studies have evaluated dropout once CBT has been initiated. For example, in randomized controlled trials (Haby, Donnelly, Corry, & Vos, 2006), the mean attrition rate for panic disorder is 19% (range 0–54%), for generalized anxiety disorder 7.8% (range 0–17%), and for depression 11.4% (range 0–37%). In the treatment of childhood anxiety disorders, attrition has been reported as 23% (e.g., Pina, Silverman, Weems, Kurtines, & Goldman, 2003). Most investigations fail to find differences between "completers" and "noncompleters" in terms of starting levels of symptoms or sociodemographics, although limited power to detect differences may be problematic here. However, Oei and Kazmierczak (1997) reported that those who dropped from group CBT for depression participated less during therapy sessions than did completers. As described elsewhere, participation in CBT, particularly in the early phase of treatment, may be mediated by expectancy for change (e.g., Westra et al., 2007). Interestingly, the addition of pharmacotherapy to CBT often results in more dropouts than does CBT alone (e.g., Furukawa, Watanabe, & Churchill, 2007), which may reflect the attribution effects described previously.

As already noted, severity and complexity of initial presentation are predictors of lesser than usual improvement with CBT (e.g., Haby, Donnelly, Corry, & Vos, 2006). Severity and complexity encompass features such as symptom severity, comorbid Axis II syndromes, medical complications, and life stressors. On the other hand, CBT that successfully treats a specific disorder has been shown to lead to improvements in surrounding comorbidity (e.g., Brown & Barlow, 1995; Craske et al., 2007).

MECHANISM DATA: ROLE OF CHANGES IN COGNITION

The cognitive appraisal model presumes that the active therapeutic mechanism is change in dysfunctional assumptions and core beliefs in the direction of being more rational or evidence based. However, the available evidence regarding mechanisms raises serious questions about the role of changes to the *content* of conscious cognition. Longmore and Worrell (2007) reviewed the evidence pertaining to the degree to which direct explicit modification of maladaptive cognitions is necessary or sufficient for CBT. They first examined component analysis studies, in which cognitive strategies were compared to behavioral strategies and their combination. While relatively few in number and only pertaining to the treatment of anxiety and depression, the conclusion was that in neither case was there strong evidence that cognitive approaches produced better results than behavioral approaches (i.e., exposure therapy and behavioral activation) alone, or that cognitive approaches added benefit to behavioral approaches. Publications since their review confirm this conclusion. That is, in their meta-analyses, Norton and Price (2007) found no differences across cognitive therapy, exposure therapy, relaxation, or their combination for anxiety disorders. In a recent meta-analysis of 17 randomized control trials for the treatment of depression, behavioral therapy conducted without explicit cognitive strategies was found to be equally effective as CBT (Ekers, Richards, & Gilbody, 2008). Finally, in an investigation of depression, differences between cognitive therapy and behavioral activation for depression were minor (Dobson et al., 2008).

Thus, despite the occasional superiority of cognitively based treatments over behavioral treatment alone (e.g., social phobia; Clark et al., 2006), the findings for no differences are broad and compelling and have led several researchers to conclude that the cognitive component of CBT is superfluous and unnecessary (e.g., Hayes, 2004). Notably, there is an alternative conclusion, which is that whereas cognitive therapy may not add substantially to the effects of behavioral therapy, cognitive therapy in its own right remains an effective treatment. Hence, clients and clinicians can choose between two effective treatment approaches—behavioral therapy and cognitive therapy. As was suggested by Borkovec and colleagues (2002), each approach may tap into a different part of the system to affect change.

Longmore and Worrell (2007) suggested a couple of reasons why cognitive therapy techniques did not significantly add to behavioral techniques. First, the majority of outcome variance may be attributed to shared, nonspecific treatment effects between the two treatments. Second, the measures of outcome may be insufficiently sensitive to detect differences between the treatment conditions. Another possibility is that in attempting to evaluate the component parts of CBT, the effectiveness of each part is diluted. For example, in comparing exposure therapy alone to exposure plus cognitive restructuring, the second condition may be weakened by the reduced amount of attention given to exposure incurred as a result of having to attend to cognitions. Furthermore, limited sample sizes of most studies to date may have limited the power to detect group differences.

Yet another possibility has been emphasized throughout this book— that cognitive therapy is as effective as behavioral therapy and does not add significantly to the effects of behavioral therapy because cognitive and behavioral approaches are essentially overlapping treatments that share procedures and mechanisms. For example, as outlined in preceding sections, cognitive therapy typically includes direct behavioral steps, including behavioral experimentation as a tool for gathering evidence, which clearly overlaps with more behaviorally oriented treatments. Furthermore, learning theory mechanisms may well be evoked by the same behavioral steps that are presumed within cognitive therapy to effect change through disconfirming misconstruals. That is, behavioral experimentation intended to gather disconfirming evidence may also serve to change reinforcement patterns, lead to habituation, and develop new inhibitory expectancies at the experiential level. Also, learning theory mechanisms may be evoked through the verbal discussion component of cognitive therapy. For example, as described earlier, logical empiricism may serve to devalue the potency of the US and thereby contribute to extinction (Cracknell & Davey, 1988; White & Davey, 1989): learning to think about social rejection in a less negative way may contribute to extinction of conditional fear responses to social situations. Also, Boyd and Levis (1983) argued that by discussing and imagining feared stimuli, cognitive therapy represents a degraded form of exposure that allows the processes of habituation, extinction, and mastery (that are presumed to mediate exposure-based approaches) to occur. Conversely, shifts in conscious cognitive appraisals may derive from behavioral reinforcement strategies (e.g., shaping assertive behaviors) and exposure-based procedures (e.g., exposure to feared situations). For example, by repeatedly expressing assertive behaviors, beliefs about oneself and the world may become more positive.

To this end, it is not surprising that shifts in cognitive appraisals are produced by both cognitive and behavioral methods of intervention (e.g., Feske & Chambless, 1995; Jacobson et al., 1996). Indeed, cognitions change as a result of pharmacotherapy approaches as well (e.g., McManus, Clark, & Hackmann, 2000). Garratt and colleagues (2007) similarly concluded from their review of pharmacotherapies and CBT for depression that more studies show no differences than show differences in the amount of cognitive change produced. However, they caution that some of these studies may not have been sufficiently powered to detect differences, and raise the possibility that cognitive change as a result of cognitive therapy is "deeper" than cognitive change as a result of pharmacotherapy. This possibility was based on the evidence that those treated with pharmacotherapy remain more cognitively reactive to depressed mood than those treated with cognitive therapy, and cognitive reactivity is a predictor of relapse (Segal et al., 1999, 2006).

Change in cognition alone is not an indicator of causal agency. Tests of mediation are required, in which change in cognition is observed as a predictor of subsequent change in symptom outcomes. A few studies report such effects. From their review, Hollon and DeRubeis (2004) concluded that changes in cognition during cognitive therapy predicted changes in symptoms. Similarly, Hofmann (2004) found that pre- to posttreatment changes in the cognitive variable of "estimated social cost" mediated reductions in social anxiety in socially anxious individuals treated with CBT. Also, Kendall and Treadwell (2007) found that changes in anxious self-statements mediated treatment gains in children with anxiety disorders undergoing CBT.

However, there are other examples where cognitive mediation is not found. In the investigation by Jacobson and colleagues (1996) of cognitive and behavioral activation treatments for depression, change in cognition in the cognitive treatment did not predict later changes in symptoms.

Similarly, Burns and Spangler (2001) found no evidence of a mediational link between dysfunctional attitudes and changes in anxiety and depression among a sizable sample (n = 521) of CBT-treated outpatients. Furthermore, Jarrett, Vittengl, Doyle, and Clark (2007) found that changes in depressive symptoms explained changes in cognition rather than vice versa. Thus, Longmore and Worrell (2007) concluded that the empirical evidence for cognitive mediation of therapeutic change is weak.

Kazdin (2007) added further reason for concern by noting that a number of studies indicate change in symptoms relatively early in treatment (e.g., Crits-Christoph et al., 2001; Tang & DeRubeis, 1999), before cognitive change strategies are fully implemented. As much as 60% to 80% of symptom change occurs by the fourth CBT session for a number of disorders (e.g., Ilardi & Craighead, 1999). Moreover, a number of studies have established that early improvement in CBT for anxiety and depression is a predictor of overall outcomes (Westra, Dozois, & Marcus, 2007). Ilardi and Craighead (1994) suggested that early response is mediated by hope, or motivation for change and the belief that one can affect change. The role of hope as a mediator of early treatment response does not necessarily negate the role of cognitive change in the later portions of treatment. Indeed, Hayes and colleagues (2007) analyzed narratives from depressed patients going through an exposure-based CBT and concluded that while early response was mediated by hope, later response was mediated by cognitive emotional processing. However, the fact that the majority of symptom response occurs in the first part of treatment without cognitive mediation suggests that if cognitive mediation does play a role later on, its role is significantly less than whatever is mediating the initial response.

These types of results led Kazdin to conclude, "Perhaps we can state more confidently now than before that whatever may be the basis for changes with CT [cognitive therapy], it does not seem to be the cognitions as originally proposed" (2007, p. 8). Part of the difficulty in establishing cognitive mediation is that the concepts themselves are problematic. Cognitive therapies of all types have been criticized for lack of conceptual clarity, lack of clear operationalization of concepts, and shifting conceptualizations and terminology over time. For example, what precisely is a "schema," and how is it best measured? Moreover, what aspects of schema should be changing throughout treatment and how is that measured? Is it that original schemas are changed, or deactivated, or are new schemas formed? Without clarity at this level, tests of mediation remain problematic.

Measures of the purported constructs are problematic as well. By far the majority of studies of cognitive mediation rely on self-report questionnaires about beliefs, such as the Thoughts Rating Form to measure catastrophic cognitions about panic attacks (e.g, Hofmann et al., 2007), and the Dysfunctional Attitude Scale to measure depressive beliefs (e.g., Jarrett et al., 2007). It is questionable whether self-report is a valid measure of cognition. For example, self-report scales may be influenced by demand characteristics to respond in a certain way. Also, Smith and Allred (1986) and Zurawski and Smith (1987) found that measures of irrational beliefs had higher correlations with measures of distress than with each other, reflecting the limited validity of such self-report measures. Finally, and importantly, the likelihood that endorsement on self-report questionnaires matches ongoing, moment-to-moment thinking and its correlation with ongoing changes in affect is questionable (Jarrett et al., 2007). There is a need for experience (in the moment) sampling of cognition and/or more objective measures, such as lexical decision tasks, that are less susceptible to responder biases. Mogg and colleagues (2001) therefore assert that much of the scientific evidence in support of the basic assumptions of CBT—the existence and influence of core schemas and beliefs and their modification by logical empiricism—is plagued by methodological problems and that the assumptions are in need of further elucidation and support.

HOW DOES CBT WORK WITH DIVERSE CLIENTS?

The empirical support for CBT derives almost entirely from studies with white middle class Europeans or Westerners. In general, CBT is aligned with European and North American values of change, self-disclosure, independence and autonomy, and rational thinking, all of which are at odds with values of harmony, family and collectivism, and spirituality that define many other cultures. Culturally sensitive CBT takes into account the cultural influences that place constraints upon the goals and methods of CBT. For example, assertiveness training may be problematic for individuals who are not expected to be assertive in their own culture or at least may need to be modified to better reflect familial or hierarchical cultural values. Behavioral activation and behavioral contracting similarly may be modified so that goals of independence and autonomy are cast within, and not at conflict with, cultural values that emphasize family and collectivism. REBT, with its emphasis on individuality and self-control, may conflict with those values as well. The willingness to engage in exposure therapy may differ depending on the amount of discrimination that individuals perceive from health care providers in general (Miranda, Nakamura, & Bernal, 2003). In addition, whereas CBT typically aims to modify overly negative self-statements, such self-criticism may be viewed as a motivator to achieve in other cultures, such as Chinese cultures (Hwang & Wood, 2007). Furthermore, cognitive therapy may be modified for cultures that emphasize balance and indirect causes of events rather than reductionist cause-and-effect relations. That is, the method by which cognitive restructuring is most effectively implemented may differ across cultures, with Western culture being more suited to single overriding alternative interpretations of a given event and Eastern culture being more suited to two or more simultaneous explanations that can be invoked depending on the context (Hofmann, 2006).

To make these adaptations requires cultural sensitivity and competency, or having the cultural self-awareness, knowledge, and skills that facilitate the delivery of effective services to ethnically and culturally diverse clients. Frameworks have been proposed for how to adapt CBT to different cultures, such as for Chinese Americans (Hwang, 2006), and descriptions of the cultural adaptation of CBT for a variety of problem areas are emerging (e.g., Hays & Iwamasa, 2006).

The effectiveness of CBT with diverse clientele is early in its research development. The extant literature was extensively reviewed in 2005 by Miranda and colleagues.[1] Most studies test cultural adaptations of existing CBT programs. Including the modifications to CBT strategies described previously, adaptations are made to the process of CBT delivery, such as provision of CBT in native languages, administration of written materials, and provision of extra services such as child care. For child and adolescent depression, the review indicated a lack of studies that evaluate outcomes across different ethnic groups. However, culturally sensitive applications of CBT have been found to be successful within certain cultural groups, such as Latino adolescents living in Puerto Rico. In terms of anxiety in youths and adolescents, there is work demonstrating the efficacy of CBT for low-income African American adolescents. Also, African American and Latino youths have been found to respond no differently than Caucasian youths to CBT for anxiety.

Behavioral contingency management for attention deficit hyperactive disorders has been evaluated in different ethnic groups: ethnic minority families have the same rates of engagement and satisfaction with the behavioral treatment as nonminority families but remain more severe at posttreatment than nonminorities. However, these differences are no longer significant after controlling for socioeconomic disadvantage, suggesting that the differences are due to socioeconomic status rather than cultural group. Behavioral interventions such as parent training for oppositional and conduct disorders have been shown to be as effective in decreasing conduct disorders in Latino children as in Caucasian children, and in African American, Latino, and Asian American compared to Caucasian children. Thus, Miranda and colleagues (2005) concluded that behavioral treatments and CBT for anxiety, depression, attention deficit hyperactivity disorders, and conduct type disorders are as effective in African American and Latino youths as in Caucasian youths.

In terms of adults, a number of studies have demonstrated the effectiveness of CBT for depression in different ethnic minority groups. Combining CBT with clinical case management results in better outcomes than CBT alone for Spanish-speaking participants who are depressed, whereas African Americans benefit more from CBT alone. Latino and African American low-income depressed women respond well to CBT that

---

[1] The results of the review are described herein without full citation of each study due to space limitations.

is modified by using culturally sensitive methods to encourage women to enter care, and by provision of babysitting and transportation. Furthermore, CBT is as cost effective for the treatment of depression in predominantly low income minority women compared to community referral.

For adult anxiety, despite occasional reports of less improvement in African Americans, most studies find equivalent treatment outcomes across groups of African American and White Americans. For example, cognitive trauma therapy has been shown to be equally effective for white and ethnic minority women with posttraumatic stress disorder.

A few studies have evaluated specific minority groups in terms of CBT for psychosis. A behavioral family management program for psychosis in low-income, Spanish-speaking populations has been shown to have poorer outcomes for less acculturated patients. The results were interpreted to suggest that a highly structured intervention may be experienced as intrusive and stressful by less-acculturated families. Elsewhere, Chinese patients who received psychoeducational intervention for psychosis along with medication were shown to achieve better gains than those who received medication only.

Overall, Miranda and colleagues (2005) concluded that CBT results do seem to generalize to African American and Latino populations, although the data for other minority groups is very sparse, and the results are limited to only a subset of the full range of psychological disorders and conditions. The degree to which interventions need to be culturally adapted is unclear, as tests comparing adapted and unadaptive versions of CBT in minority groups are not yet available. Nonetheless, one would assume that in the course of a good functional analysis, issues that pertain to the sociocultural context and that are relevant to minority group status would be addressed, in the same way that they would be for nonminority individuals. As Miranda and colleagues state, "Thus, knowledge of the culture and context and the capacity to distinguish between what may be culturally adaptive versus pathological are minimal considerations of culturally competent care" (2005, p. 134).

6

Future Developments

Cognitive–behavioral therapy (CBT) is one of today's most practiced and researched therapies, which means it is constantly evolving. This chapter discusses the future of CBT, including the contributions of cognitive psychological research, mindfulness as a technique, and the gaps that remain in establishing the efficacy and effectiveness of CBT.

FUNCTION VERSUS CONTENT OF COGNITION

In contrast to behavioral theories and therapies, cognitive theory and therapy initially developed without strong science or theoretical foundations. The science of cognitive psychology developed in relative isolation of cognitive theories and therapies, and only recently have the two met. In some ways, the science of cognitive psychology provides support for the premises of cognitive therapy. As an example, cognitive science has illuminated the attentional biases to threat, memory biases, and distortions in appraisals of ambiguous information that characterize persons with anxiety and depression (e.g., Mathews & MacLeod, 2005). These biases are the target of cognitive therapy. However, the restriction of cognitive therapy to *conscious* appraisals as the target of intervention is problematic in light of the science of cognition, which now demonstrates that by far the majority of information processing occurs at subconscious levels, without conscious appraisal.

Cognitive psychologists have long recognized two cognitive systems, one that is automatic and out of awareness and the other that is conscious and more effortful.[1] More specifically, most cognitive processing has the potential to include large amounts of information and takes place rapidly and without awareness. Brewin (1996) asserted that we become aware of the products of such unaware processing in the form of thoughts and images. The unaware aspect of cognitive processing is believed to be heavily influenced by prior learning and to be activated almost innately (Brewin, 1996). In contrast, conscious processing is slow and deliberate, but also flexible and adaptable. Brewin argues that the different cognitive and behavioral techniques work at different levels of processing. Cognitive therapies emphasize verbally accessible knowledge in the form of conscious assessments of the meaning and causes of events, whereas behavioral therapies have the potential through direct experience to influence processes that occur without awareness. Hence, the degree to which a logico-deductive challenging of negative cognitions (i.e., cognitive therapy) is sufficient for managing the vast majority unconscious processing is questioned (e.g., McNally, 1994). In response to these types of concerns with the cognitive reappraisal model, attention has been given to alternative treatment approaches.

Teasdale and colleagues have led this movement in the treatment for depression. Teasdale and Barnard (1993) proposed a model for how information is processed, called the interacting cognitive subsystems model, which draws largely from cognitive science. In this model, higher-level propositional processes represent specific, explicit meanings that map directly onto language. In contrast, implicational processes represent generic and holistic levels of intuitive meaning that do not directly map onto language. Instead, they reflect the "felt sense" of experience. Furthermore, only the implicational meaning processes are directly linked to emotion. However, cognitive therapy clearly is targeted at the propositional

---

[1] This distinction is recognized in the later versions of Beck's cognitive therapy (e.g., Clark, Beck, & Alford, 1999).

processes. Hence, Teasdale (1993) criticizes cognitive appraisal models for being primarily concerned with specific meanings or beliefs. He argues that targeting such propositional processes may be insufficient as a means for shifting emotion and thus advocates that in addition to targeting specific meanings (as in cognitive therapy), holistic meanings be addressed. The latter are addressed through nonevidential interventions such as guided imagery and mindful experiencing.

Mindfulness

For these reasons, Teasdale and colleagues investigated the effects of mindfulness.

> The mindful state is characterized by direct experience of current reality "in the moment" rather than elaborative, ruminative thinking about one's situation, and its origins, implications and associations. Mindfulness training appears to be associated with a reduction in the tendency to "float away" into ruminative, elaborative thought streams. Such training would be expected to reduce the tendency of those prone to depressive relapse to become locked into the ruminative cognitive cycles that, we have suggested, play such an important role in relapse. (Teasdale, Segal, & Williams, 1995, p. 34)

Mindfulness is viewed as particularly helpful for "nipping in the bud" the escalation of mild states of negative affect at points of potential relapse, whereas direct cognitive therapy is considered more valuable for the more intense problems associated with episodes of major depression.

Williams and colleagues have continued this line of research and have tested mindfulness-based cognitive therapy, which is a group treatment that incorporates mindfulness-based stress reduction (Kabat-Zinn, 1990). In this model, dysfunctional cognitions are treated as events to be observed rather than targets to be challenged and restructured. In this way, the cognitions become decentered from the self, which in turn is believed to result in them having less impact on emotions. Mindfulness-based cognitive therapy has been shown to be effective in reducing risk of relapse in depressed persons (e.g., Teasdale et al., 2000) and treatment-resistant depressed clients (e.g., Kenny & Williams, 2007).

Acceptance and Commitment Therapy

Acceptance and decentering approaches to dysfunctional cognitions are core to another behavioral treatment, called acceptance and commitment therapy (Hayes, 1994). Acceptance and commitment therapy is based on relational frame theory (Hayes et al., 1999), which is a "post-Skinnerian" contextual behavioral theory about how language influences cognition, emotion, and behavior. According to this model, believing that one must control and respond to language (i.e., verbalizations, thoughts, self-talk, catastrophizing) leads to increasingly limited opportunities for valued action.

Within acceptance and commitment therapy, rigid attempts to control aversive internal states, also referred to as experiential avoidance, are considered counterproductive relative to acceptance of emotions (Eifert & Heffner, 2003). Hayes (1994) defined acceptance as the conscious abandonment of a direct change agenda in private events and openness to experiencing thoughts and emotions as they are. According to Hayes and Pankey (2003), the methods for acceptance involve detecting and challenging experiential avoidance (i.e., recognizing the dysfunctionality of attempting to control internal private experiences); encouraging aware, flexible, and open exposure to previously avoided events (as is done through exposure therapy but with an approach of deliberately exploring feelings throughout the exposure); encouraging the development of new responses in the presence of previously avoided events (e.g., observing characteristics of a previously feared situation that had not been detected previously); and defusion techniques (such as mindfulness) to distance oneself from private verbal events that lead to verbal entanglement.

To expand behavior, acceptance and commitment therapy helps clients alter the functional significance of action-limiting language. Therefore, a central component is teaching cognitive defusion skills, which involve distancing oneself from the literal meaning and content of language. Clients are encouraged to use these skills, which are taught via experiential exercises such as mindful observation and use of metaphors (i.e., nonlinear language), whenever language thwarts action in valued life directions. Thus, the goal is not changing cognitions or symptoms, as in CBT, but rather mindful tolerance and acceptance of cognitions and symptoms. Within acceptance and commitment therapy, behavior alone and not cognition is targeted for content change.

Beyond cognitive defusion, additional components of acceptance and commitment therapy include creative hopelessness, or helping clients to recognize that their past efforts to change, control, or evade aversive emotional states and negative thoughts have not worked and have led them to avoid, limit, and/or undermine valued life activities. Values-based exercises, such as writing the epitaph for one's imagined tombstone, help clients to unearth and examine life values. Behavioral willingness or committed action involves choosing to behave in ways that are consistent with chosen values, in the face of painful thoughts and feelings that may arise (Hayes et al., 1999).

Dialectical Behavior Therapy

The notion of acceptance appears within the context of other treatments as well, including Linehan's (1994) dialectical behavior therapy. Dialectical behavior therapy emphasizes the balance between acceptance and change. Linehan defines acceptance as the active process of orienting to private experience moment by moment. Her approach to treatment, designed specifically for individuals with borderline personality disorder features, integrates change-oriented behavioral strategies, such as skills training, contingency management, and problem solving, with acceptance and validation-based strategies. In addition, some problem behaviors may be accepted while other problem behaviors are targeted for change. Therapists balance acceptance-based styles of communicating, using warmth and genuineness, with directive and sometimes offbeat, change-based styles of communicating. Clients are encouraged to move from "either-or" thinking to "both-and" thinking. Rather than attempt to directly dispute or challenge negative self-statements, the dialectical behavior therapy approach might help clients to recognize their thoughts as another behavior, validate those thoughts where appropriate, and then provide a perspective of change as well. Metaphors are used to encourage dialectical thinking, as a way of facilitating an observer role, and noticing or embracing paradoxes is encouraged.

Function Over Content

In summary, these particular behavioral and cognitive–behavioral therapies are regarding not just the content (and sometimes not the content at all) but rather the function of cognition. Notably, this is how cognition is managed within behavioral activation treatments for depression and other behavioral interventions that derive from instrumental conditioning principles. Hence, rather than rely on conscious reappraisal efforts to change the content of cognitions, these treatments focus on ways of lessening the impact of cognition on emotions and behaviors by decentering or acceptance, without attempting to change cognition. The results indicate that such an approach lessens the relapse rate for depression (Teasdale et al., 2002). However, there is need for much more research on mindfulness and acceptance-based approaches for a wider array of disorders and the combination with or comparison to traditional CBT.

INCORPORATE ADVANCES IN LEARNING THEORY

The value of cognitive science and its implications for cognitive theory and therapy is matched by the need for behaviorists to remain up-to-date with the latest advances in behavioral science. In so doing, the technology of behavioral treatments can be realigned with the basic science, in the way it was when behavior therapy was first developed. The latest advances generate some exciting possibilities for maximizing learning during exposure therapy. One possibility derives from the facilitative effect of multiple excitatory CSs during extinction training (Rescorla, 2001). This is called "deepened extinction" and is presumed to result in superior learning because of the potency of the mismatch with expectancies provided by the presence of more than one CS relative to a single CS alone. There have been no direct investigations of this topic in clinical samples. However, the concept of deepened extinction is easily translated into exposure therapy; indeed, this method is employed in the treatment for panic disorder and agoraphobia when interoceptive exposure to feared physiological sensations (e.g., elevated heart rate) and in vivo exposure to feared situations (e.g., walking through a shopping mall) are subsequently combined (e.g., drinking caffeinated substances while walking through a shopping mall; Barlow & Craske, 1988). Given the important clinical implications, direct investigation of deepened extinction in clinical samples is needed.

Another interesting development is the use of biological agents to facilitate the consolidation of inhibitory learning during extinction. Fear extinction is dependent on NMDA-type glutamate receptors, or NMDAr (reviewed in Walker & Davis, 2002). NMDAr inhibitors block extinction when given systemically or infused directly into the amygdala during extinction training. Furthermore, systemic or intra-amygdala treatments with d-cycloserine (DCS), an agonist at the glycine binding site of the NMDA receptor, facilitate extinction in rodents (Walker & Davis, 2002), although not completely (Vervliet, 2008). Some investigations have combined DCS with exposure therapy for phobias. The results to date remain somewhat mixed, with several reports of enhancement of exposure therapy and one report of no effects (see Vervliet, 2008). Nonetheless, further evaluation of enhancement of learning throughout exposure therapy by biological agents clearly is warranted.

Advances have been made in the neurobiology of fear learning and extinction, with attention to three general structures: the amygdala, the prefrontal cortex (PFC), and the hippocampus (see Sotres-Bayon, Cain, & LeDoux, 2006, for a review). The PFC has long been implicated in executive control and decision making. Recent work has revealed that certain parts of the PFC (i.e., ventral medial) are also responsible for emotional regulation and, in particular, the ability to interpret emotional stimuli and change behavior accordingly (Sotres-Bayon et al., 2006). Also, extinction in nonprimates is associated with neuronal activity primarily within the medial PFC (e.g., Rauch, Shin, & Phelps, 2006). Research with humans similarly shows that changes in the medial PFC occur during extinction (e.g., Gottfried & Dolan, 2004). One possibility, therefore, is that during extinction testing, the PFC exerts inhibitory control over the amygdala. Behavioral methods for enhancing the PFC throughout exposure therapy may prove to be a useful direction for future research. Conceivably, when cognitive restructuring does enhance the benefits of exposure therapy alone, it may be doing so by activation of the PFC. Further investigation of the neurobiology underlying cognitive therapy in the context of extinction-based exposure strategies is needed.

Finally, research indicates ways of increasing the accessibility and retrievability of exposure-based learning once treatment is over (see Craske et al., 2008, for a review). For example, in general, retention of learned nonemotional material is enhanced by random and variable practice. Studies in phobic samples have shown that exposure to varied phobic stimuli (e.g., multiple spiders) leads to better maintenance of treatment gains at follow-up than exposure to a constant stimulus (e.g., a single spider); and random and variable exposure to feared situations produces superior outcomes in comparison to the traditional blocked and constant method of exposure. Also, bridging the context of treatment with contexts outside of treatment may enhance the retrieval of inhibitory associations once the treatment is over (Bouton, Garcia-Gutierrez, Zilski, & Moody, 2006). One such bridge is to instruct participants to recall the exposure therapy context, which has been shown to decrease return of fear (see Craske et al., 2008). Bridging from the extinction to renewal context also can be provided by objects that serve as retrieval cues (Bouton et al., 2006). In rodents, retrieval cues during extinction trials attenuate context-based renewal effects, more so even than relatively novel cues or cues that were present during conditioning rather than extinction. The benefits of retrieval cues have been demonstrated in human samples; specifically, the return of reactivity to alcohol cues is reduced by use of retrieval cues (see review by Craske et al., 2008). The continued exploration of ways of enhancing new learning and its retrieval at a later time is an important direction and necessary to keep the technology of behavioral strategies in line with the science of learning and memory.

EFFICACY AND EFFECTIVENESS RESEARCH

A number of topics warrant further research. As described previously, there is a strong need for more methodologically rigorous research on the mechanisms or mediators of CBT. Knowledge about mediators will contribute to optimization of the delivery of CBT. Another area is long-term outcomes from CBT and ways of enhancing the maintenance of treatment gains. As noted previously, behavioral manipulations can offset return of fear following exposure therapy for phobias and thereby improve long-term outcomes. However, there is a need for ways to maintain CBT outcomes more broadly as well. Methodologies might include following the acute phase of CBT with phone-delivered or Internet-based booster sessions, which have been found in at least one study to contribute to long-term outcomes (Craske et al., 2006). In addition, mindfulness-based interventions are showing promise for reducing relapse following treatment for depression (Teasdale et al., 2002).

Further research is needed to assess the extent to which CBT differs from other active treatment conditions, such as psychodynamic or interpersonal therapies, since most extant comparative research compares CBT to no-treatment or nondirective supportive counseling conditions. Moreover, methods for optimizing the combination of CBT with pharmacological approaches warrant much more investigation, as do issues pertaining to attrition, its prediction, and its prevention. Unified CBT protocols, designed to manage negative affect more broadly than existing protocols that target specific problem areas, is another important topic (Allen, McHughs, & Barlow, 2008).

Another area is the implementation of CBT in real-world settings. Effectiveness research remains in its infancy. There exist only a few benchmarking studies by which results in community settings and samples are compared to the results obtained by research investigations. Nonetheless, existing data are promising (e.g., Levitt et al., 2007). Effectiveness studies have also demonstrated the efficacy of CBT relative to treatment as usual in primary care settings (e.g., Roy-Byrne et al., 2005). A number of questions remain open to more investigation, such as the level of training that is required for therapists to be sufficiently competent in delivering CBT. At the same time, further consideration should be given to methods of delivery that involve minimal therapist involvement, as a way of increasing the availability of CBT to those in need. Ongoing research using computer-assisted and Internet-based delivery of CBT provides an interesting avenue in this regard. Furthermore, effectiveness research that addresses culturally sensitive adaptations to CBT is sorely needed.

Finally, research attention could be more fully directed to the utility of CBT as a preventative intervention. Some headway already has been made in this regard, such as the school-based universal prevention program, known as FRIENDS (Lowry-Webster, Barrett, & Dadds, 2001). This CBT program has been found to lower self-reported anxiety compared to an untreated control, for unselected children ages 10 to 13. Barrett and Turner (2001) found that the results were equally effective whether the FRIENDS program was led by a psychologist or a teacher who received one day of training. A number of other studies show the benefits of CBT for individuals with risk factors for, or initial symptoms of, disorders. This includes risk for depression (Seligman, Schulman, DeRubeis, & Hollon, 1999) and panic disorder (e.g., Gardenswartz & Craske, 2001).

7

Summary

Cognitive–behavioral therapy (CBT) is an amalgam of behavioral and cognitive intervention strategies that are derived from learning and cognitive theory and that share the philosophy of an empirical science approach to treatment implementation and evaluation. CBT has evolved from a purely behavioral form at its inception to become a behavioral and cognitive approach. The origins were classical conditioning and instrumental conditioning learning theories. Translation of those theories into treatments was spurred by mental health needs following World War II and by dissatisfaction with psychoanalytic approaches. The need for treatment constructs that were observable and measurable, and thereby falsifiable in the experimental sense, were strongly emphasized. In the 1950s, the principles of classical conditioning were translated into treatments for anxiety disorders, pioneered largely by Wolpe, and then extended to treatments for substance use disorders as well as others. These treatments centered on ways of weakening, or extinguishing, maladaptive CRs. At around the same time, the principles of instrumental conditioning were translated into treatments for severe behavior problems, led by the efforts of Skinner and colleagues. These treatments centered on ways of changing antecedents and consequences to decrease maladaptive behaviors and increase adaptive ones. The development of standardized behavioral treatment procedures led to a burgeoning of treatment outcome studies and dissemination to practicing clinicians throughout the 1960s and 1970s.

However, there was some dissatisfaction with the strictly behavioral approach, particularly for the treatment for depression. The astute clinical observations of Ellis and Beck in the late 1950s and 1960s led them to independently propose a new model of therapy that emphasized the content of conscious cognition, thereby providing the "content" to behavior therapy. Their treatment models emphasized the role of distorted or irrational thinking and ways of disputing or disconfirming that thinking through logical discussion, in order to develop more rational and less distorted ways of thinking. The acceptance of the cognitive approach was facilitated by a number of factors, including the value given to behavioral technologies within cognitive approaches.

In addition, a paradigmatic shift was occurring in the context of learning theory. Early conditioning models failed to ascribe a causal role to cognition. However, learning theorists, such as Tolman and Rescorla, recognized the role of expectancies in both instrumental learning and classically conditioned responding. Furthermore, Bandura's social learning theory viewed higher-level cognition as a critical determinant of behavior and emotions. Thus, a "cognitive revolution" of learning theories occurred separately from but alongside the development of cognitive therapies.

These developments allowed a complementary melding of cognitive and learning theories. For example, cognition in the form of expectancies is now judged to be central to learning through reinforcement (instrumental learning) or through association (classical conditioning). Conversely, instrumental and classical conditioning are presumed to produce cognitions that in turn may then mediate future learning experiences. For this reason, the array of cognitive and behavioral intervention strategies, even though primarily derived from either learning theory models or cognitive theory models, typically can be explained by principles from both models. That is, cognitive therapy, which is intended to identify and modify maladaptive self-statements and beliefs, can be explained by principles of learning theory. Behavioral strategies, which are intended to modify antecedents and consequences of instrumental voluntary behaviors and to weaken CRs, can be explained by changes in cognitions. The melding of cognitive and learning theories and procedures underlies the contemporary approach to CBT.

CBT is regarded as the most empirically supported psychosocial treatment, and its effects carry across a wide array of disorders. It is also very popular, with some surveys showing that the majority of clinicians regard themselves as ascribing to a CBT orientation. Popularity is due not only to the demonstrated effectiveness of CBT but also its problem-focused and time-limited nature, as well as its availability in manualized form. However, optimal delivery of CBT requires an understanding not just of the manualized procedures to be implemented but the underlying principles. One of the goals of this book is to explicate the principles underlying the various cognitive and behavioral interventions. That being said, positive effects are obtained from CBT even when it is delivered by inexperienced therapists and even with no therapist contact at all, as in Internet-administered programs, a finding that attests to the value of the strategies themselves.

Caveats certainly exist and there is always room for improvement. More research is needed, for example, on ways of reducing attrition and for improving long-term outcomes. Other areas in need of further development are dissemination, including cultural adaptation of CBT, and its use as a preventative intervention for individuals at risk.

The original behavioral approach developed from an existing empirical science and theory of learning. In contrast, the cognitive therapy approach developed from clinical observation; the science of cognition developed separately from cognitive therapy. While the science of cognition has yielded some support for the premises of cognitive therapy, it has also resulted in questions about a therapy that focuses on conscious cognitive reappraisal as its primary agent of change. That is, recognition that much of cognitive processing occurs without conscious awareness and in a way that is not amenable to logical reasoning has led to concerns about the adequacy of purely cognitive appraisal methods and mechanisms. These concerns are matched by lack of good evidence for therapeutic change to be mediated by changes in conscious cognition, although insensitive methodology may be a limiting factor. Consequently, new movements are occurring within the field of CBT. Specifically, attention is being given to the role of mindfulness and acceptance, strategies that focus less on the content of conscious cognition and more on the function of cognition. This is coupled with advances in the science of learning that are now being translated into ways of optimizing treatment. Thus, CBT is considered to be now in its third wave of evolution. Such a change represents a hallmark feature of CBT, a treatment approach that is guided by empirical science, and is updated as scientific advancements are made.

Glossary of Key Terms

ACCEPTANCE AND COMMITMENT THERAPY   A therapy developed by Hayes and colleagues that emphasizes acceptance of internal states and commitment toward behavioral change for reaching life goals.

ACTIVITY CHART   A chart to assess current levels of activity and the connection between activity and mood.

ANTECEDENT   An event that precedes a targeted behavior, emotion. or cognition.

APPETITIVE CLASSICAL CONDITIONING   The development of conditional responses based on associations of conditional stimuli with innately positive unconditional stimuli.

ARBITRARY INFERENCE   A type of cognitive error.

AVERSIVE CLASSICAL CONDITIONING   The development of conditional responses based on associations of conditional stimuli with innately aversive unconditional stimuli.

BEHAVIORAL ACTIVATION   A treatment approach for depression that increases positive reinforcement and decreases avoidance behaviors.

BEHAVIORAL CONTRACTING   A statement of a set of behaviors to be followed and the related positive and negative consequences to be carried out conditionally on compliance or noncompliance with the plan; also referred to as contingency contracting.

BEHAVIORAL EXPERIMENTATION   A cognitive therapy strategy involving behavioral practice designed to gather information that disconfirms distortions in thinking; also referred to as hypothesis testing.

BEHAVIORAL REHEARSAL   A reinforcement-based strategy for shaping and developing behaviors.

BREATHING RETRAINING   A skill comprised of slow breathing rate and diaphragmatic versus thoracic breathing.

CLASSICAL CONDITIONING   Developing conditional responses to previously neutral stimuli as a result of associations with innately evocative unconditional stimuli.

COGNITIVE CONTENT SPECIFICITY   Concept that each affective state and psychological disorder has its own specific cognitive profile and that cognitive content determines the type of emotional disturbance.

COGNITIVE DEFUSION TECHNIQUES   A component of acceptance and commitment therapy that aims to help to distance oneself from private verbal events or the meaning and content of language.

COGNITIVE ERROR   An error in thinking.

COGNITIVE REHEARSAL   Practice replacing irrational thoughts with rational ones.

COGNITIVE RESTRUCTURING   A set of techniques for identifying maladaptive thoughts and beliefs and replacing them with more evidence-based thoughts and beliefs.

CONDITIONAL RESPONSE   A learned response to a conditional stimulus as a function of its association with an innately evocative stimulus.

CONDITIONAL STIMULUS   A previously neutral stimulus that, through association with an unconditional stimulus, produces a conditional response.

CONSEQUENCE   An event that follows a behavior and influences the occurrence or form of that behavior.

COVERT SENSITIZATION   A procedure that aims to reduce maladaptive behaviors by pairing them with aversive events in imagery.

CUE EXPOSURE   Exposure to substance-related cues to extinguish conditional responses to the cues.

DIALECTICAL BEHAVIOR THERAPY   A therapy developed by Linehan that focuses on the balance between acceptance and change.

DICHOTOMOUS THINKING   A type of cognitive error involving considering only the extremes.

DISTANCING   A cognitive technique of learning to view one's thoughts more objectively and to treat them as hypotheses rather than facts.

DOWNWARD ARROW TECHNIQUE   A cognitive therapy technique in which the consequences of a particular thought are repeatedly drawn out to the final meaning.

ESTABLISHING OPERATIONS   Events or biological conditions that alter the effects of reinforcing or punishing consequences.

EXPOSURE THERAPY   A set of procedures for systematically and repeatedly confronting stimuli, such as feared stimuli in the case of anxiety disorders or drug-related stimuli in the case of substance use disorders

EXTINGUISH   To lessen a conditional response through the absence of the unconditional stimulus or through the absence of consequences.

FLOODING EXPOSURE   Prolonged and continuous exposure to highly anxiety-provoking stimuli.

FUNCTIONAL ANALYSIS   An analysis of the causal relations among cognitions, behaviors, emotions, and environmental and cultural contexts.

HABIT REVERSAL   A set of procedures for decreasing nervous habits and tics and a range of repetitive behaviors that are controlled by self-stimulation.

HABITUATION   Decreased response strength as a function of repeated exposure to a stimulus.

HIERARCHY   A list of activities or situations, ordered from least to most difficult, to be repeatedly faced in exposure therapy.

HOMEWORK   Assignments or practices to be carried out between treatment sessions.

HYPOTHESIS TESTING   A cognitive therapy approach, also referred to as behavioral experimentation, involving behavioral practices designed to gather data that disconfirms distortions in thinking.

INHIBITORY LEARNING   The development of inhibitory associations or expectancies about a conditional stimulus; that the conditional stimulus no longer predicts the unconditional stimulus.

INSTRUMENTAL CONDITIONING   Influencing or modifying voluntary behaviors as a function of their consequences.

INTEROCEPTIVE EXPOSURE   Repeated and systematic exposure to feared bodily sensations.

IRRATIONAL BELIEFS   According to Ellis, these are beliefs that are not likely to be supported or confirmed by the environment and lead to inappropriate negative emotions in the face of difficulty.

LOGICAL EMPIRICISM   A cognitive therapy strategy for evaluating the evidence as a way of either supporting or disconfirming appraisals.

MINDFULNESS   A set of strategies for learning to observe without judging, acceptance or openness to experience, and abandonment of attempts to change private events.

OPERANT BEHAVIOR   Behavior that operates on the environment and is maintained by its consequences.

OUTCOME EXPECTANCY   Beliefs about the likelihood and valence of events.

OVERGENERALIZATION   A type of cognitive error involving viewing a single instance as being indicative of a broader class of events.

PERSONAL SCIENTIST PERSPECTIVE   Being an objective observer of one's own reactions.

PROBLEM SOLVING   A set of skills for identifying problems and generating potential solutions and action plans for managing problems.

PROGRESSIVE MUSCLE RELAXATION   A set of procedures developed by Jacobson for relaxing muscle tension, conducted progressively throughout the body.

PUNISHER   A consequence that causes a behavior to occur with less frequency.

RATIONAL BELIEFS   According to Ellis, these are beliefs that promote survival and happiness; they are likely to find empirical support in the environment and to lead to appropriate behavioral and emotional responses to difficulties.

RATIONAL DISPUTATION   A set of techniques, pioneered by Ellis, for disputing irrational thoughts.

RATIONAL–EMOTIVE BEHAVIOR THERAPY   A cognitive therapy developed by Albert Ellis that aims to dispute irrational thoughts and replace them with rational thoughts.

RECIPROCAL DETERMINISM   Reciprocal influences among behaviors, cognitions, and environmental factors that continuously influence each other.

REINFORCER   A consequence that causes a behavior to occur with greater frequency.

RESPONSE PREVENTION   A behavioral strategy for blocking avoidance behaviors, often applied to compulsions.

RULE-GOVERNED BEHAVIOR   Behavior that is not controlled by environmental antecedents or consequences but instead is controlled by verbally stated rules.

SAFETY SIGNAL   A stimulus that predicts the absence of the aversive unconditional stimulus, also referred to as a conditional inhibitor.

SCHEMA   An internal set of beliefs about the self and the world that is used to perceive, code, and recall information.

SELF-EFFICACY   Conviction that one can successfully execute a behavior required to produce an outcome.

SELF-INSTRUCTION TRAINING   A set of procedures developed by Donald Meichenbaum, involving overt and then covert self-statements for dealing with difficult situations.

SELF-MONITORING   Observing and recording the occurrence and functional relations among thoughts, behaviors, and emotions as they occur.

SHAPING   The use of reinforcement to develop low-frequency or new behaviors.

SKILLS TRAINING   A set of instrumentally based procedures for developing new behaviors.

SOCIAL LEARNING THEORY   The incorporation of cognition as a critical determinant of learning, spearheaded by Rotter and Bandura.

SOCRATIC QUESTIONING   A technique used in cognitive therapy to facilitate the client's own discovery of errors in thinking and different ways of thinking.

STIMULUS CONTROL   When a behavior occurs in the presence of a particular stimulus and not in its absence.

SYSTEMATIC DESENSITIZATION   A set of procedures developed by Wolpe, in which relaxation is used as a counterconditioner to reciprocally inhibit anxiety associated with feared images.

THERAPIST MODELING   When the therapist demonstrates a specific behavior or cognition to be imitated by the client.

THIRD WAVE BEHAVIORAL THERAPIES   Behavioral therapies that emphasize the function rather than the cognitive content of cognitions.

UNCONDITIONAL STIMULUS   An innately evocative stimulus, either aversive or appetitive.

UNIFIED PROTOCOLS   CBT for a broad array of negative emotions, cognitions, and behaviors.

VIRTUAL REALITY EXPOSURE   Exposure using the technology of virtual reality.

Suggested Readings

Barlow, D. H. (Ed). (2008). *Clinical handbook of psychological disorders. New York:* Guilford Press.

Clark. D. M., & Fairburn, C. G. (Eds.). (1997). *Science and practice of cognitive behaviour therapy.* Oxford, England: Oxford University Press.

Farmer, R. F., & Chapman, A. L. (2008). *Behavioral interventions in cognitive behavior therapy: Practical guidance for putting theory into action.* Washington, DC: American Psychological Association.

Hays, P. A., & Iwamasa, G. Y. (2006). *Culturally responsive cognitive–behavioral therapy: Assessment, practice, and supervision.* Washington, DC: American Psychological Association.

Hersen, M. (Ed.). (2002). *Clinical behavior therapy.* New York: Wiley.

Miranda, J., Bernal, G., Lau, A., Kohn, L., Hwang, W., & LaFromboise, T. (2005). State of the science on psychosocial interventions for ethnic minorities. *Annual Review of Clinical Psychology, 1,* 113–142.

O'Donohue, W., Fisher, J. E., & Hayes S. C. (Eds.). (2003). *Cognitive behavior therapy: Applying empirically supported techniques in your practice.* Hoboken, NJ: Wiley.

References

Addis, M. E., & Jacobson, N. S. (2000). A closer look at the treatment rationale and homework compliance in cognitive–behavioral therapy for depression. *Cognitive Therapy and Research, 24*(3), 313–326.

Allen, L. B., McHugh, R. K., & Barlow, D. H. (2008). Emotional disorders: A unified approach. In D. H. Barlow (Ed.), *Clinical handbook of psychological disorders: A step-by-step treatment manual* (4th ed., pp. 216–249). New York: Guilford Press.

American Psychological Association. (2005). *Policy statement on evidence-based practice in psychology.* Retrieved December 15, 2006, from http://www2.apa.org/practice/abpstatement.pdf

Azrin, N. H., & Nunn, R. G. (1974). A rapid method of eliminating stuttering by a regulated breathing approach. *Behaviour Research and Therapy, 12*(4), 279–286.

Bandura, A. (1969). Social learning of moral judgments. *Journal of Personality and Social Psychology, 11*(3), 275–279.

Bandura, A. (1973). Aggression: A social learning analysis. Oxford, England: Prentice Hall.

Bandura, A. (1977). Self-efficacy: Toward a unifying theory of behavioral change. *Psychological Review, 84*, 191–215.

Bandura, A. (1978). Reflections on self-efficacy. In S. Rachman (Ed.), *Perceived self-efficacy: Analysis of Bandura's theory. Advances in behavioral research and therapy, 1*, 237–269.

Bandura, A. (1988). Self-efficacy conception of anxiety. *Anxiety Research, 1*, 77–98.

Barlow, D. H., & Craske, M. G. (1988). The phenomenology of panic. In S. Rachman & J. D. Maser (Eds.), *Panic: Psychological perspectives* (pp. 11–35). Hillsdale, NJ: Erlbaum.

Barrett, P., Farrell, L., Dadds, M., & Boulter, N. (2005). Cognitive–behavioral family treatment of childhood obsessive-compulsive disorder: Long-term follow-up and predictors of outcome. *Journal of the American Academy of Child & Adolescent Psychiatry, 44*(10), 1005–1014.

Barrett, P., & Turner, C. (2001). Prevention of anxiety symptoms in primary school children: Preliminary results from a universal school-based trial. *British Journal of Clinical Psychology, 40*(4), 399–410.

Basoglu, M., Marks, I. M., Kilic, C., Swinson, R. P., Noshirvani, H., Kuch, K., et al. (1994). Relationship of panic, anticipatory anxiety, agoraphobia and global improvement in panic disorder with agoraphobia treated with alprazolam and exposure. *British Journal of Psychiatry, 164*(5), 647–652.

Beck, A. T. (1963). Thinking and depression. *Archives of General Psychiatry, 9,* 324–333.

Beck, A. T. (1976). *Cognitive therapy and the emotional disorders.* New York: International Universities Press.

Beck, A. T. (1993). Cognitive therapy: Past, present, and future. *Journal of Consulting and Clinical Psychology, 61,* 194–198.

Beck, A. T. (2005). The current state of cognitive therapy: A 40-year retrospective. *Archives of General Psychiatry, 62*(9), 953–959.

Beck, A. T., & Clark, D. A. (1997). An information processing model of anxiety: Automatic and strategic processes. *Behaviour Research and Therapy, 35,* 49–58.

Beck, A. T., Rush, A. J., Shaw, B. F., & Emery, G. (1979). *Cognitive therapy of depression.* New York: Guilford Press.

Bernstein, D. A., & Borkovec, T. D. (1973). *Progressive relaxation training: A manual for the helping professions.* Champaign, IL: Research Press.

Borkovec, T. D., Abel, J. L., & Newman, H. (1995). Effects of psychotherapy on comorbid conditions in generalized anxiety disorder. *Journal of Consulting and Clinical Psychology, 63*(3), 479–483.

Borkovec, T. D., Newman, M. G., Pincus, A. L., & Lytle, R. (2002). A component analysis of cognitive-behavioral therapy for generalized anxiety disorder and the role of interpersonal problems. *Journal of Consulting and Clinical Psychology, 70*(2), 288–298.

Bouton, M. E., Garcia-Gutierrez, A., Zilski, J., & Moody, E. W. (2006). Extinction in multiple contexts does not necessarily make extinction less vulnerable to relapse. *Behaviour Research and Therapy, 44*(7), 983–994.

Bouton, M. E., Woods, A. M., Moody, E. W., Sunsay, C., & Garcia-Gutierrez, A. (2006). Counteracting the context-dependence of extinction: Relapse and tests of some relapse prevention methods. In M. G. Craske, D. Hermans, & D. Vansteenwegen (Eds.), *Fear and learning: From basic processes to clinical implications* (pp. 175–196). Washington, D C: American Psychological Association.

Boyd, T. L., & Levis, D. J. (1983). Exposure is a necessary condition for fear-reduction: A reply to de Silva and Rachman. *Behaviour Research and Therapy, 21*(2), 143–149.

Brewin, C. R. (1996). Theoretical foundations of cognitive–behavior therapy for anxiety and depression. *Annual Review of Psychology, 47*, 33–57.

Brosan, L., Reynolds, S., & Moore, R. G. (2007). Factors associated with competence in cognitive therapists. *Behavioural and Cognitive Psychotherapy, 35*, 179–190.

Brosan, L., Reynolds, S., & Moore, R. G. (2008). Self-evaluation of cognitive therapy performance: Do therapists know how competent they are? *Behavioural and Cognitive Psychotherapy, 36*, 581–587.

Brown, T. A., & Barlow, D. H. (1995). Long-term outcome in cognitive–behavioral treatment of panic disorder: Clinical predictors and alternative strategies for assessment. *Journal of Consulting and Clinical Psychology, 63*, 754–765.

Burns, D. D. (1980). *Feeling good: The new mood therapy.* New York: Morrow.

Burns, D. D., & Spangler, D. L. (2000). Does psychotherapy homework lead to improvements in depression in cognitive-behavioral therapy or does improvement lead to increased homework compliance? *Journal of Consulting and Clinical Psychology, 68*(1), 46–56.

Burns, D. D., & Spangler, D. L. (2001). Do changes in dysfunctional attitudes mediate changes in depression and anxiety in cognitive behavioral therapy? *Behavior Therapy, 32*(2), 337–369.

Butler, A. C., Chapman, J. E., Forman, E. M., & Beck, A. T. (2006). The empirical status of cognitive–behavioral therapy: A review of meta-analyses. *Clinical Psychology Review, 26*, 17–31.

Cautela, J. R. (1967). Covert sensitization. *Psychological Reports, 20*, 459–468.

Cerny, J. A., Barlow, D. H., Craske, M. G., & Himadi, W. G. (1987). Couples treatment of agoraphobia: A two-year follow-up. *Behavior Therapy, 18*(4), 401–415.

Chambless, D. L., & Ollendick, T. H. (2001). Empirically supported psychological interventions: Controversies and evidence. *Annual Review of Psychology, 52*, 685–716.

Clark, D. A., Beck, A. T., & Alford, B. A. (1999). *Scientific foundations of cognitive theory and therapy of depression.* Hoboken, NJ: Wiley.

Clark, D. M., Ehlers, A., Hackmann, A., McManus, F., Fennell, M., Grey, N., et al. (2006). Cognitive therapy versus exposure and applied relaxation in social phobia: A randomized controlled trial. *Journal of Consulting and Clinical Psychology, 74*(3), 568–578.

Clark, D. M., & Fairburn, C. G. (1997). *Science and practice of cognitive behaviour therapy.* New York: Oxford University Press.

Collins, B. N., & Brandon, T. H. (2002). Effects of extinction context and retrieval cues on alcohol cue reactivity among nonalcoholic drinkers. *Journal of Consulting and Clinical Psychology, 70,* 390–397.

Conoley, C. W., Padula, M. A., Payton, D. S., & Daniels, J. A. (1994). Predictors of client implementation of counselor recommendations: Match with problem, difficulty level, and building on client strengths. *Journal of Counseling Psychology, 41,* 3–7.

Cote, G., Gauthier, J. G., Laberge, B., Cormier, H. J., & Plamondon, J. (1994). Reduced therapist contact in the cognitive behavioral treatment of panic disorder. *Behavior Therapy, 25,* 123–145.

Cracknell, S., & Davey, G. C. (1988). The effect of perceived unconditioned response strength on conditioned responding in humans. *Medical Science Research, 16*(4), 169–170.

Craske, M. G., & Barlow, D. H. (2008). Panic disorder and agoraphobia. In D. H. Barlow (Ed.), *Clinical handbook of psychological disorders* (4th ed.). New York: Guilford Press.

Craske, M. G., Farchione, T. J., Allen, L. B., Barrios, V., Stoyanova, M., & Rose, R. (2007). Cognitive behavioral therapy for panic disorder and comorbidity: More of the same or less of more? *Behaviour Research and Therapy, 45*(6), 1095–1109.

Craske, M. G., Kircanksi, K., Zelikowsky, M., Mystkowski, J., Chowdhury, N., & Baker, A. (2008). Optimizing inhibitory learning during exposure therapy. *Behaviour Research and Therapy, 46*(1), 5–27.

Craske, M. G., Roy-Byrne, P., Stein, M. B., Sullivan, G., Hazlett-Stevens, H., Bystritsky, A., et al. (2006). CBT intensity and outcome for panic disorder in a primary care setting. *Behavior Therapy, 37*(2), 112–119.

Craske, M. G., & Tsao, J. C. I. (1999). Self-monitoring with panic and anxiety disorders. *Psychological Assessment, 11,* 466–479.

Crits-Christoph, P., Connolly, M. B., Gallop, R., Barber, J. P., Tu, X., Gladis, M., et al. (2001). Early improvement during manual-guided cognitive and dynamic psychotherapies predicts 16-week remission status. *Journal of Psychotherapy Practice & Research, 10*(3), 145–154.

Davey, G. C. L. (2006). Cognitive mechanisms in fear acquisition and maintenance. In M. G. Craske, D. Hermans, & D. Vansteenwegen (Eds.), *Fear and learning: From basic processes to clinical implications* (pp. 99–116). Washington, DC: American Psychological Association.

Dewey, D., & Hunsley, J. (1990). The effects of marital adjustment and spouse involvement on the behavioral treatment of agoraphobia: A meta-analytic review. *Anxiety Research, 2*(2), 69–83.

Dimidjian, S., Hollon, S. D., Dobson, K. S., Schmaling, K. B., Kohlenberg, R. J., Addis, M. E., et al. (2006). Randomized trial of behavioral activation, cognitive therapy, and antidepressant medication in the acute treatment of adults with major depression. *Journal of Consulting and Clinical Psychology, 74,* 658–670.

Dobson, K. S., Hollon, S. D., Dimidjian, S., Schmaling, K. B., Kohlenberg, R. J., Gallop, R. J., et al. (2008). Randomized trial of behavioral activation, cognitive therapy, and antidepressant medication in the prevention of relapse and recurrence in major depression. *Journal of Consulting and Clinical Psychology, 76,* 468–477.

Dow, M. G. (1994). Social inadequacy and social skills. In L. W. Craighead, W. E. Craighead, A. E. Kazdin, & M. J. Mahoney (Eds.), *Cognitive and behavioral interventions: An empirical approach to mental health problems* (pp. 123–140). Boston: Allyn & Bacon.

Durham, R. C., Chambers, J. A., Power, K. G., Sharp, D. M., Macdonald, R. R., Major, K. A., et al. (2005). Long-term outcome of cognitive behaviour therapy clinical trials in central Scotland. *Health Technology Assessment, 9,* 1–174.

D'Zurilla, T. J., & Nezu, A. M. (1999). *Problem-solving therapy: A social competence approach to clinical intervention* (2nd ed.). New York: Springer.

Edelman, R. E., & Chambless, D. L. (1995). Adherence during sessions and homework in cognitive-behavioral group treatment of social phobia. *Behaviour Research and Therapy, 33,* 573–577.

Eelen, P., & Vervliet, B. (2006). Fear conditioning and clinical implications: What can we learn from the past? In M. G. Craske, D. Hermans, & D. Vansteenwegen (Eds.), *Fear and learning: From basic processes to clinical implications* (pp. 17–35). Washington, DC: American Psychological Association.

Eifert, G. H., Forsyth, J. P., & Schauss, S. L. (1993). Unifying the field: Developing an integrative paradigm for behavior therapy. *Journal of Behavior Therapy & Experimental Psychiatry, 24,* 107–118.

Eifert, G. H., & Heffner, M. (2003). The effects of acceptance versus control contexts on avoidance of panic-related symptoms. *Journal of Behavior Therapy and Experimental Psychiatry, 34*(3–4), 293–312.

Ekers, D., Richards, D., & Gilbody, S. (2008). A meta-analysis of randomized trials of behavioural treatment of depression. *Psychological Medicine, 38,* 611–623.

Ellis, A. (1957). Outcome of employing three techniques of psychotherapy. *Journal of Clinical Psychology, 13,* 344–350.

Ellis, A. (1962). *Reason and emotion in psychotherapy.* New York: Lyle Stuart.

Ellis, A. (2003). Cognitive restructuring of the disputing of irrational beliefs. In W. O'Donohue, J. E. Fisher, & S. C. Hayes (Eds.), *Cognitive behavior therapy: Applying empirically supported techniques in your practice* (pp. 79–83). Hoboken, NJ: Wiley.

Eysenck, H. J. (1952). The effects of psychotherapy: An evaluation. *Journal of Consulting Psychology, 16,* 319–324.

Eysenck, H. J. (Ed.). (1960). *Behavior therapy and the neuroses.* Oxford, England: Pergamon.

Fairburn, C. G., Cooper, Z., Shafran, R., & Wilson, G. T. (2008). Eating disorders: A transdiagnostic protocol. In D. H. Barlow (Ed.), *Clinical handbook of psychological disorders* (4th ed., pp. 578–614). New York: Guilford Press.

Farmer, R. F., & Chapman, A. L. (2008). *Behavioral interventions in cognitive behavior therapy.* Washington, DC: American Psychological Association.

Feeley, M., DeRubeis, R. J., & Gelfand, L. A. (1999). The temporal relation of adherence and alliance to symptom change in cognitive therapy for depression. *Journal of Consulting and Clinical Psychology, 67,* 578–582.

Ferguson, K. E. (2003). Relaxation. In W. O'Donohue, J. E. Fisher, & S. C. Hayes (Eds.), *Cognitive behavior therapy: Applying empirically supported techniques in your practice* (pp. 330–340). Hoboken, NJ: Wiley.

Feske, U., & Chambless, D. L. (1995). Cognitive behavioral versus exposure only treatment for social phobia: A meta-analysis. *Behavior Therapy, 26*(4), 695–720.

Foa, E. B., & Kozak, M. J. (1986). Emotional processing of fear: Exposure to corrective information. *Psychological Bulletin, 99,* 20–35.

Foa, E. B., & McNally, R. J. (1996). Mechanisms of change in exposure therapy. In R. M. Rapee (Ed.), *Current controversies in the anxiety disorders* (pp. 329–343). New York: Guilford Press.

Foa, E. B., Steketee, G., Grayson, J. B., Turner, R. M., & Latimer, P. (1984). Deliberate exposure and blocking of obsessive-compulsive rituals: Immediate and long-term effects. *Behavior Therapy, 15,* 450–472.

Foa, E. B., Zoellner, L., Feeny, N. C., Meadows, E., & Jaycox, L. (2000, November). *Evaluation of a brief cognitive-behavioral program for the prevention of chronic PTSD in recent assault victims.* Paper presented at the 34th Annual Convention of the Association for the Advancement of Behavior Therapy, New Orleans, LA.

Ford, T. E., & Kruglanski, A. W. (1995). Effects of epistemic motivations on the use of accessible constructs in social judgment. *Personality and Social Psychology, 21*(9), 950–962.

Furukawa, T. A., Watanabe, N., & Churchill, R. (2007). Combined psychotherapy plus antidepressant for panic disorder with or without agoraphobia: Systematic review. *Cochrane database of systematic reviews,* (1), CD004364.

Gardenswartz, C. A., & Craske, M. G. (2001). Prevention of panic disorder. *Behavior Therapy, 32*(4), 715–737.

Garratt, G., Ingram, R. E., Rand, K. L., & Sawalani, G. (2007). Cognitive processes in cognitive therapy: Evaluation of the mechanisms of change in the treatment of depression. *Clinical Psychology: Science and Practice, 14,* 224–239.

Garssen, B., de Ruiter, C., & van Dyck, R. (1992). Breathing retraining: A rational placebo? *Clinical Psychology Review, 12*(2), 141–153.

Goldfried, M. R. (1971). Systematic desensitization as training in self-control. *Journal of Consulting and Clinical Psychology, 37*(2), 228–234.

Goldfried, M. R., & Davison, G. C. (1994). *Clinical behavior therapy.* New York: Wiley.

Gottman, J., Notarius, C., Markman, H., Bank, S., Yoppi, B., & Rubin, M. E. (1976). Behavior exchange theory and marital decision making. *Journal of Personality and Social Psychology, 34*(1), 14–23.

Gottfried, J. A., & Dolan, R. J. (2004). Human orbitofrontal cortex mediates extinction learning while accessing conditioned representations of value. *Nature Neuroscience, 7*(10), 1144–1152.

Greenberg, L. S., & Safran, J. D. (1989). Emotion in psychotherapy. *American Psychologist, 44,* 19–29.

Haaga, D. A. F., & Davison, G. C. (1993). An appraisal of rational–emotive therapy. *Journal of Consulting and Clinical Psychology, 61,* 215–220.

Haby, M. M., Donnelly, M., Corry, J., & Vos, T. (2006). Cognitive behavioural therapy for depression, panic disorder and generalized anxiety disorder: A meta-regression of factors that may predict outcome. *Australian and New Zealand Journal of Psychiatry, 40*(1), 9–19.

Hahlweg, K., Fiegenbaum, W., Frank, M., Schroeder, B., & von Witzleben, I. (2001). Short- and long- term effectiveness of an empirically supported treatment for agoraphobia. *Journal of Consulting and Clinical Psychology, 69*(3), 375–382.

Hayes, A. M., Feldman, G. C., Beevers, C. G., Laurenceau, J.-P., Cardaciotto, L., & Lewis-Smith, J. (2007). Discontinuities and cognitive changes in an exposure-based cognitive therapy for depression. *Journal of Consulting and Clinical Psychology, 75*(3), 409–421.

Hayes, S. C. (1994). Content, context, and the types of psychological acceptance. In S. C. Hayes, N. S. Jacobson, V. M. Follette, & M. J. Dougher (Eds.), *Acceptance and change: Content and context in psychotherapy* (pp. 13–32). Reno, NV: Context Press.

Hayes, S. C. (2004). Acceptance and commitment therapy, relational frame theory, and the third wave of behavior therapy. *Behavior Therapy, 35,* 639–665.

Hayes, S. C. (2008). Climbing our hills: A beginning conversation on the comparison of acceptance and commitment therapy and traditional cognitive behavioral therapy. *Clinical Psychology: Science and Practice, 15*(4), 286–295.

Hayes, S. C. & Pankey, J. (2003). Acceptance. In W. O'Donohue, J. Fisher, & S. C. Hayes (Eds.), *Cognitive behavior therapy: Applying empirically supported techniques in your practice* (pp. 4–9). Hoboken, NJ: Wiley.

Hayes, S. C., Strosahl, K. D., & Wilson, K. G. (1999). *Acceptance and commitment therapy: An experiential approach to behavior change.* New York: Guilford Press.

Hays, P. A., & Iwamasa, G. Y. (2006). *Culturally responsive cognitive–behavioral therapy: Assessment, practice, and supervision.* Washington, DC: American Psychological Association.

Hecker, J. E., Losee, M. C., Roberson-Nay, R., & Maki, K. (2004). Mastery of your anxiety and panic and brief therapist contact in the treatment of panic disorder. *Journal of Anxiety Disorders, 18,* 111–126.

Heide, F. J., & Borkovec, T. D. (1983). Relaxation-induced anxiety: Paradoxical anxiety enhancement due to relaxation training. *Journal of Consulting and Clinical Psychology, 51*(2), 171–182.

Heidt, J. M., & Marx, B. P. (2003). Self-monitoring as a treatment vehicle. In W. O'Donohue, J. E. Fisher, & S. C. Hayes (Eds.), *Cognitive behavior therapy: Applying empirically supported techniques in your practice* (pp. 361–367). New York: Wiley.

Hendriks, G. J., Oude Voshaar, R. C., Keijsers, G. P., Hoogduin, C. A., & van Balkom, A. J. (2008). Cognitive–behavioral therapy for late-life anxiety disorders: A systematic review and meta-analysis. *Acta Psychiatrica Scandinavica, 117,* 403–411.

Hofmann, S. G. (2004). Cognitive mediation of treatment change in social phobia. *Journal of Consulting and Clinical Psychology, 72*(3), 392–399.

Hofmann, S. G. (2006). The importance of culture in cognitive and behavioral practice. *Cognitive and Behavioral Practice, 13*(4), 243–245.

Hofmann, S. G., Meuret, A. E., Rosenfield, D., Suvak, M. K., Barlow, D. H., Gorman, J. M., et al. (2007). Preliminary evidence for cognitive mediation during cognitive-behavioral therapy of panic disorder. *Journal of Consulting and Clinical Psychology, 75*(3), 374–379.

Holden, A. E., O'Brien, G. T., Barlow, D. H., Stetson, D., & Infantino, A. (1983). Self-help manual for agoraphobia: A preliminary report of effectiveness. *Behavior Therapy, 14,* 545–556.

Hollon, S. D., & DeRubeis, R. J. (2004). Effectiveness of treatment for depression. In R. L. Leahy (Ed.), *Contemporary cognitive therapy: Theory, research, and practice* (pp. 45–61). New York: Guilford Press.

Houmanfar, R., Maglieri, K. A., & Roman, H. R. (2003). Behavioral contracting. In W. O'Donohue, J. E. Fisher, & S. C. Hayes (Eds.), *Cognitive behavior therapy: Applying empirically supported techniques in your practice* (pp. 40–45). Hoboken, NJ: Wiley.

Hull, C. L. (1943). *Principles of behavior.* New York: Appleton-Century-Crofts.

Huppert, J. D., Bufka, L. F., Barlow, D. H., Gorman, J. M., Shear, M. K., & Woods, S. W. (2001). Therapists, therapist variables, and cognitive–behavioral therapy outcome in a multicenter trial for panic disorder. *Journal of Consulting and Clinical Psychology, 69,* 747–755.

Hwang, W. (2006). The psychotherapy adaptation and modification framework: Application to Asian Americans. *American Psychologist, 61,* 702–715.

Hwang, W., & Wood, J. (2007). Being culturally sensitive is not the same as being culturally competent. *Pragmatic Case Studies in Psychotherapy, 3,* 44–50.

Ilardi, S. S., & Craighead, W. E. (1994). The role of nonspecific factors in cognitive-behavioral therapy for depression. *Clinical Psychology: Science and Practice, 1*(2), 138–156.

Ilardi, S. S., & Craighead, W. E. (1999). Rapid early response, cognitive modification, and nonspecific factors in cognitive behavior therapy for depression: A reply to Tang and DeRubeis. *Clinical Psychology: Science and Practice, 6*(3), 295–299.

Iosifescu, D. V., Nierenberg, A. A., Alpert, J. E., Smith, M., Bitran, S., Dording, C., et al. (2003). The impact of medical comorbidity on acute treatment in major depressive disorder. *American Journal of Psychiatry, 160*(12), 2122–2127.

Issakidis, C., & Andrews, G. (2004). Pretreatment attrition and dropout in an outpatient clinic for anxiety disorders. *Acta Psychiatrica Scandinavica, 109*(6), 426–433.

Jacobson, E. (1938). *Progressive muscle relaxation.* Chicago: University of Chicago Press.

Jacobson, N. S., Dobson, K. S., Truax, P. A., Addis, M. E., Koerner, K., Gollan, J. K., et al. (1996). A component analysis of cognitive–behavioral treatment for depression. *Journal of Consulting and Clinical Psychology, 64*(2), 295–304.

Jacobson, N. S., Martell, C. R., & Dimidjian, S. (2001). Behavioral activation treatment for depression: Returning to contextual roots. *Clinical Psychology: Science and Practice, 8*(3), 255–270.

James, I. A., Blackburn, I. M., Milne, D. L., & Reichfelt, F. K. (2001). Moderators of trainee therapists' competence in cognitive therapy. *British Journal of Clinical Psychology, 40*, 131–141.

Jarrett, R. B., Vittengl, J. R., Doyle, K., & Clark, L. A. (2007). Changes in cognitive content during and following cognitive therapy for recurrent depression: Substantial and enduring, but not predictive of change in depressive symptoms. *Journal of Consulting and Clinical Psychology, 75*(3), 432–446.

Jones, M. C. (1924). A laboratory study of fear: The case of Peter. *Pedagogical Seminary, 31*, 308–315.

Kabat-Zinn, J. (1990). *Full catastrophe living: Using the wisdom of your body and mind to face stress, pain, and illness.* New York: Dell.

Kazantzis, N., Deane, F. P., & Ronan, K. R. (2002). *Study of systematic homework administration: Research manual for therapists at Waitemata District Health Boards Cognitive Therapy Center (Cognitive Therapy Center Research Programme, Vol. 1).* Albany, New Zealand: Massey University.

Kazdin, A. E. (2007). Mediators and mechanisms of change in psychotherapy research. *Annual Review of Clinical Psychology, 3*, 1–27.

Kazdin, A. E., Marciano, P. L., & Whitley, M. K. (2005). The therapeutic alliance in cognitive-behavioral treatment of children referred for oppositional, aggressive, and antisocial behavior. *Journal of Consulting and Clinical Psychology, 73*(4), 726–730.

Keijsers, G. P. J., Schaap, C. P. D. R., Hoogduin, C. A. L., & Lammers, M. W. (1995). Patient-therapist interaction in the behavioral treatment of panic disorder with agoraphobia. *Behavior Modification, 19*, 491–517.

Kendall, P. C. (1993). Cognitive-behavioural therapies with youth: Guiding theory, current status and emerging developments. *Journal of Consulting and Clinical Psychology, 61*, 235–247.

Kendall, P. C., & Treadwell, K. R. (2007). The role of self-statements as a mediator in treatment for youth with anxiety disorders. *Journal of Consulting and Clinical Psychology, 75*, 380–389.

Kenny, M. A., & Williams, J. M. (2007). Treatment-resistant depressed patients show a good response to mindfulness-based cognitive therapy. *Behaviour Research and Therapy, 45,* 617–625.

Kirsch, I., Lynn, S. J., Vigorito, M., & Miller, R. R. (2004). The role of cognition in classical and operant conditioning. *Journal of Clinical Psychology, 60*(4), 369–392.

Kraft, A. R., & Hoogduin, C. A. (1984). The hyperventilation syndrome: A pilot study on the effectiveness of treatment. *British Journal of Psychiatry, 145,* 538–542.

Kraus, C. A., Kunik, M. E., & Stanley, M. A. (2007). Use of cognitive behavioral therapy in late-life psychiatric disorders. *Geriatrics, 62,* 21–26.

Laidlaw, K., Davidson, K., Toner, H., Jackson, G., Clark, S., Law, J., et al. (2008). A randomised controlled trial of cognitive behaviour therapy vs. treatment as usual in the treatment of mild to moderate late life depression. *International Journal of Geriatric Psychiatry, 23,* 843–850.

Lang, P. J. (1971). The application of psychophysiological methods to the study of psychotherapy and behavior modification. In A. E. Bergin & S. L. Garfield (Eds.), *Handbook of psychotherapy and behavior change: An empirical analysis* (pp. 75–125). New York: Wiley.

Lang, P. J., Melamed, B. G., & Hart, J. (1970). A psychophysiological analysis of fear modification using an automated desensitization procedure. *Journal of Abnormal Psychology, 76*(2), 220–234.

Lavallee, Y. J., Lamontagne, G., Pinard, G., Annable, L., & Tetreault, L. (1977). Effects of EMG biofeedback, diazepam and their combination on chronic anxiety. *Journal of Psychosomatic Research, 21,* 65–71.

Levis, D. J. (1999). The negative impact of the cognitive movement on the continued growth of the behavior therapy movement: A historical perspective. *Genetic, Social, and General Psychology Monographs, 125,* 157–171.

Levitt, J. T., Malta, L. S., Martin, A., Davis, L., & Cloitre, M. (2007). The flexible application of a manualized treatment for PTSD symptoms and functional impairment related to the 9/11 World Trade Center attacks. *Behaviour Research and Therapy, 45*(7), 1419–1433.

Lewinsohn, P. M. (1974). A behavioral approach to depression. In R. M. Freidman & M. M. Katz (Eds.), *The psychology of depression: Contemporary theory and research* (pp. 157–185). New York: Wiley.

Lindsley, O., Skinner, B., & Solomon, H. (1953). *Studies in behaviour therapy, status report I.* Orthon, MA: Metropolitan State Hospital.

Linehan, M. M. (1994). Case consultation: A borderline dilemma. A. L. Berman (ed.) [A comment]. *Suicide and Life-Threatening Behavior, 24,* 192–198.

Longmore, R. J., & Worrell, M. (2007). Do we need to challenge thoughts in cognitive behavior therapy? *Clinical Psychology Review, 27*(2), 173–187.

Lovibond, P. F., Davis, N. R., & O'Flaherty, A. S. (2000). Protection from extinction in human fear conditioning. *Behaviour Research and Therapy, 38,* 967–983.

Lowry-Webster, H. M., Barrett, P. M., & Dadds, M. R. (2001). A universal prevention trial of anxiety and depressive symptomatology in childhood: Preliminary data from an Australian study. *Behaviour Change, 18*(1), 36–50.

Martell, C. R. (2003). Behavioral activation treatment for depression. In W. O'Donohue, J. E. Fisher, & S. C. Hayes (Eds.), *Cognitive behavior therapy: Applying empirically supported techniques in your practice* (pp. 28–32). Hoboken, NJ: Wiley.

Martin, G., & Pear, J. (2003). *Behavior modification: What it is and how to do it* (7th ed.). Upper Saddle River, NJ: Prentice Hall.

Mathews, A., & MacLeod, C. (2005). Cognitive vulnerability to emotional disorders. *Annual Review of Clinical Psychology, 1*(1), 167–195.

McCabe, R. E., & Antony, M. M. (2005). Panic disorder and agoraphobia. In M. M. Antony, D. R. Ledley, & R. G. Heimberg (Eds.), *Improving outcomes and preventing relapse in cognitive-behavioral therapy* (pp. 1–37). New York: Guilford Press.

McCrady, B. S. (2008). Alcohol use disorders. In D. H. Barlow (Ed.), *Clinical handbook of psychological disorders: A step-by-step treatment manual* (4th ed., pp. 492–546). New York: Guilford Press.

McFall, R. M., & Marston, A. R. (1970). An experimental investigation of behavior rehearsal in assertive training. *Journal of Abnormal Psychology, 76*(2), 295–303.

McManus, F., Clark, D. M., & Hackmann, A. (2000). Specificity of cognitive biases in social phobia and their role in recovery. *Behavioural and Cognitive Psychotherapy, 28*(3), 201–209.

McNally, R. J. (1994). *Panic disorder: A critical analysis.* New York: Guilford.

Meichenbaum, D. (1977). *Cognitive behavior modification.* New York: Plenum Press.

Meyer, V. (1966). Modification of expectations in cases with obsessional rituals. *Behaviour Research and Therapy, 4,* 273–280.

Miller, C. (2002). Flooding. In M. Hersen & W. Sledge (Eds.), *Encyclopedia of psychotherapy, Vol. 1* (pp. 809–913). New York: Elsevier Science.

Miller, W. R., & Rollnick, S. (1991). *Motivational interviewing: Preparing people to change addictive behaviour.* New York: Guilford Press.

Mineka, S., & Zinbarg, R. (2006). A contemporary learning theory perspective on the etiology of anxiety disorder: It's not what you thought it was. *American Psychologist, 61*(1), 10–26.

Miranda, J., Bernal, G., Lau, A., Kohn, L., Hwang, W. C., & LaFromboise, T. (2005). State of the science on psychosocial interventions for ethnic minorities. *Annual Review of Clinical Psychology, 1*, 113–142.

Miranda, J., Nakamura, R., & Bernal, G. (2003). Including ethnic minorities in mental health intervention research: A practical approach to a long-standing problem. *Culture, Medicine and Psychiatry, 27*, 467–486.

Mogg, K., Stopa, L., & Bradley, B. P. (2001). "From the conscious into the unconscious": What can the cognitive theories of psychopathology learn from Freudian theory? *Psychological Inquiry, 12*(3), 139–143.

Myers, K. M., & Davis, M. (2007). Mechanisms of fear extinction. *Molecular Psychiatry, 12*(2), 120–150.

Naugle, A. E., & Maher, S. (2003). Modeling and behavioral rehearsal. In W. O'Donohue, J. E. Fisher, & S. C. Hayes (Eds.), *Cognitive behavior therapy: Applying empirically supported techniques in your practice* (pp. 238–246). Hoboken, NJ: Wiley.

Newman, C. F. (2003). Cognitive restructuring: Identifying and modifying maladaptive schemas. In W. O'Donohue, J. E. Fisher, & S. C. Hayes (Eds.), *Cognitive behavior therapy: Applying empirically supported techniques in your practice* (pp. 89–95). Hoboken, NJ: Wiley.

Nezu, A. M., Nezu, C. M., & Lombardo, E. (2003). Problem-solving therapy. In W. O'Donohue, J. E. Fisher, & S. C. Hayes (Eds.), *Cognitive behavior therapy: Applying empirically supported techniques in your practice* (pp. 301–307). Hoboken, NJ: Wiley.

Norton, P. J., & Price, E. C. (2007). A meta-analytic review of adult cognitive–behavioral treatment outcome across the anxiety disorders. *Journal of Nervous and Mental Disease, 195*(6), 521–531.

Oei, T. P., & Kazmierczak, T. (1997). Factors associated with dropout in a group cognitive behaviour therapy for mood disorders. *Behaviour Research and Therapy, 35*(11), 1025–1030.

Ohman, A., & Mineka, S. (2001). Fears, phobias, and preparedness: Toward an evolved module of fear and fear learning. *Psychological Review, 108*(3), 483–522.

Organista, K. C. (2006). Cognitive–behavioral therapy with Latinos and Latinas. In P. A. Hays & G. Y. Iwamasa (Eds.), *Culturally responsive cognitive–behavioral therapy: Assessment, practice, and supervision* (pp. 73–96). Washington, DC: American Psychological Association.

Pavlov, I. P. (1927).*Conditioned reflexes* (G. V. Anrep, Trans). London: Oxford University Press.

Pina, A. A., Silverman, W. K., Weems, C. F., Kurtines, W. M., & Goldman, M. L. (2003). A comparison of completers and noncompleters of exposure-based cognitive and behavioral treatment for phobic and anxiety disorders in youth. *Journal of Consulting and Clinical Psychology, 71*(4), 701–705.

Poppen, R. (1998). *Behavioral relaxation training and assessment* (2nd ed.). Thousand Oaks, CA: Sage.

Rachman, S. (1978). *Fear and courage.* San Francisco: Freeman.

Rachman, S. (1997). The evolution of cognitive behaviour therapy. In D. M. Clark & C. G. Fairburn (Eds.), *Science and practice of cognitive behaviour therapy* (pp. 3–26). New York: Oxford University Press.

Rachman, S., & Hodgson, R. S. (1980). *Obsessions and compulsions.* Englewood Cliffs, NJ: Prentice Hall.

Rachman, S. J., & Wilson, G. T. (1980). *The effects of psychological therapy.* Oxford, England: Pergamon Press.

Rains, J. C. (2008). Change mechanisms in EMG biofeedback training: Cognitive changes underlying improvements in tension headaches. *Headache, 48*(5), 736–737.

Rauch, S. L., Shin, L. M., & Phelps, E. A. (2006). Neurocircuitry models of post-traumatic stress disorder and extinction: Human neuroimaging research-past, present, and future. *Biological Psychiatry, 60*(4), 376–382.

Rescorla, R. A. (1968). Probability of shock in presence and absence of CS in fear conditioning. *Journal of Comparative & Physiological Psychology, 66,* 1–5.

Rescorla, R. A. (2001). Experimental extinction. In R. R. Mowrer & S. B. Klein (Eds.), *Handbook of contemporary learning theories* (pp. 199–154). Mahwah, NJ: Erlbaum.

Robins, C. J., & Hayes, A. M. (1993). An appraisal of cognitive therapy. *Journal of Consulting and Clinical Psychology, 61,* 205–214.

Robinson, P. (2003). Homework in cognitive behavior therapy. In W. O'Donohue, J. E. Fisher, & S. C. Hayes (Eds.), *Cognitive behavior therapy: Applying empirically supported techniques in your practice* (pp. 202–211). Hoboken, NJ: Wiley.

Roth, A. & Fonagy, P. (1996). *What works for whom? A critical review of psychotherapy research.* London: Guilford Press.

Rotter, J. B. (1954). *Social learning and clinical psychology.* Englewood Cliffs, NJ: Prentice Hall.

Roy-Byrne, P. P., Craske, M. G., Stein, M. B., Sullivan, G., Bystritsky, A., Katon, W., et al. (2005). A randomized effectiveness trial of cognitive-behavioral therapy and medication for primary care disorder. *Archives of General Psychiatry, 62*(3), 290–298.

Sanderson, W. C., & Bruce, T. J. (2007). Cause and management of treatment-resistant panic disorder and agoraphobia: A survey of expert therapists. *Cognitive and Behavioral Practice, 14,* 26–35.

Schneider, A. J., Mataix-Cols, D., Marks, I. M., & Bachofen, M. (2005). Internet-guided self-help with or without exposure therapy for phobic and panic disorders. *Psychotherapy and Psychosomatics, 74,* 154–164.

Schultz, J. H., & Luthe, W. (1959). *Autogenic training: A psychophysiologic approach to pscyhotherapy.* Oxford, England: Grune & Stratton.

Segal, Z. V., Gemar, M., & Williams, S. (1999). Differential cognitive response to a mood challenge following successful cognitive therapy or pharmacotherapy for unipolar depression. *Journal of Abnormal Psychology, 108,* 3–10.

Segal, Z. V., Kennedy, M. D., Gemar, M., Hood, K., Pedersen, R., Buis, T., et al. (2006). Cognitive reactivity to sad mood provocation and the prediction of depressive relapse. *Archives of General Psychiatry, 63,* 749–755.

Seligman, M. E. (1971). Phobias and preparedness. *Behavior Therapy, 2*(3), 307–320.

Seligman, M. E. P., Schulman, P., DeRubeis, R. J., & Hollon, S. D. (1999). The prevention of depression and anxiety. *Prevention & Treatment, 2,* Article 8.

Sherrington, C. S. (1947). *The integrative action of the central nervous system.* Cambridge, England: Cambridge University Press.

Siegel, S. (1978). Tolerance to the hyperthermic effect of morphine in the rat is a learned response. *Journal of Comparative and Physiological Psychology, 92*(6), 1137–1149.

Skinner, B. F. (1938). *The behavior of organisms: An experimental analysis.* New York: Appleton-Century-Crofts.

Skinner, B. F. (1953). *Science and human behavior.* Oxford, England: Macmillan.

Smith, G. T., Goldman, M. S., Greenbaum, P. E., & Christiansen, B. A. (1995). Expectancy for social facilitation from drinking: The divergent paths of high-expectancy and low-expectancy adolescents. *Journal of Abnormal Psychology, 104*(1), 32–40.

Smith, T. W., & Allred, K. D. (1986). Rationality revisited: A reassessment of the empirical support for the rational–emotive model. In P. C. Kendall (Ed.), *Advances in cognitive–behavioral research and therapy* (Vol. 5, pp. 63–87). New York: Academic Press.

Sotres-Bayon, F., Cain, C. K., & LeDoux, J. E. (2006). Brain mechanisms of fear extinction: Historical perspectives on the contribution of prefrontal cortex. *Biological Psychiatry, 60*(4), 329–336.

Spek, V., Cuijpers, P., Nyklicek, I., Riper, H., Keyzer, J., & Pop, V. (2007). Internet-based cognitive behaviour therapy for symptoms of depression and anxiety: A meta-analysis. *Psychological Medicine, 37,* 319–328.

Spirito, A. (1999). Empirically supported treatments in pediatric psychology. *Journal of Pediatric Psychology, 24,* 87–174.

Stewart, J., de Wit, H., & Eikelboom, R. (1984). Role of unconditioned and conditioned drug effects in the self-administration of opiates and stimulants. *Psychological Review, 91*(2), 251–268.

Stewart, R. E., & Chambless, D. L. (2007). Does psychotherapy research inform treatment decisions in private practice? *Journal of Clinical Psychology, 63*(3), 267–281.

Stobie, B., Taylor, T., Quigley, A., Ewing, S., & Salkovskis, P. M. (2007). Contents may vary: A pilot study of treatment histories of OCD patients. *Behavioural and Cognitive Psychotherapy, 35,* 273–282.

Swinson, R. P., Fergus, K. D., Cox, B. J., & Wickwire, K. (1995). Efficacy of telephone-administered behavioral therapy for panic disorder with agoraphobia. *Behaviour Research and Therapy, 33,* 465–469.

Swinson, R. P., Soulios, C., Cox, B. J., & Kuch, K. (1992). Brief treatment of emergency room patients with panic attacks. *American Journal of Psychiatry, 149*(7), 944–946.

Tang, T. Z., & DeRubeis, R. J. (1999). Reconsidering rapid early response in cognitive behavioral therapy for depression. *Clinical Psychology: Science and Practice, 6*(3), 283–288.

Task Force on Promotion and Dissemination of Psychological Procedures. (1995). Training in and dissemination of empirically-validated psychological treatments: Report and recommendations. *The Clinical Psychologist, 48,* 3–23.

Teasdale, J. D. (1993). Emotion and two kinds of meaning: Cognitive therapy and applied cognitive science. *Behaviour Research and Therapy, 31,* 339–354.

Teasdale, J. D., & Barnard, P. J. (1993). *Affect, cognition and change.* Hillsdale, NJ: Erlbaum.

Teasdale, J. D., Moore, R. G., Hayhurst, H., Pope, M., Williams, S., & Segal, Z. V. (2002). Metacognitive awareness and prevention of relapse in depression: Empirical evidence. *Journal of Consulting and Clinical Psychology, 70*(2), 275–287.

Teasdale, J. D., Segal, Z., & Williams, J. M. (1995). How does cognitive therapy prevent depressive relapse and why should attentional control (mindfulness) training help? *Behaviour Research and Therapy, 33,* 25–39.

Teasdale, J. D., Segal, Z. V., Williams, J. M., Ridgeway, V. A., Soulsby, J. M., & Lau, M. A. (2000). Prevention of relapse/recurrence in major depression by mindfulness-based cognitive therapy. *Journal of Consulting and Clinical Psychology, 68,* 615–623.

Thorndike, E. L. (1898). Animal intelligence. *Psychological Review Monograph Supplement, 2*(4, Whole No. 8).

Thorndike, E. L. (1932). *The fundamentals of learning.* New York: Teachers College Press.

Tolman, E. C. (1948). Cognitive maps in rats and men. *Psychological Review, 55,* 189–208.

Vervliet, B. (2008). Learning and memory in conditioned fear extinction: effects of d-cycloserine. *Acta Psychologica, 127*(3), 601–613.

Vittengl, J. R., Clark, L. A., Dunn, T. W., & Jarrett, R. B. (2007). Reducing relapse and recurrence in unipolar depression: A comparative meta-analysis of cognitive–behavioral therapy's effects. *Journal of Consulting and Clinical Psychology, 75,* 475–488.

Walker, D. L., & Davis, M. (2002). The role of amygdale glutamate receptors in fear learning, fear-potentiated startle, and extinction. *Pharmacology, Biochemistry and Behavior. Special Issue: Functional Role of Specific Systems Within the Extended Amygdala and Hypothalamus, 71*(3), 379–392.

Watson, J. B., & Rayner, R. (1920). Conditioned emotional reactions. *Journal of Experimental Psychology, 3,* 1–14.

Watts, F. (1971). Desensitization as an habituation phenomenon: I. Stimulus intensity as determinant of the effects of stimulus lengths. *Behaviour Research and Therapy, 9*(3), 209–217.

Weissman, M. M., Verdeli, H., Gameroff, M. J., Bledsoe, S. E., Betts, K., Mufson, L., et al. (2006). National survey of psychotherapy training in psychiatry, psychology, and social work. *Archives of General Psychiatry, 63*(8), 925–934.

Weisz, J. R., Jensen, A. L., & McLeod, B. D. (2005). Development and dissemination of child and adolescent psychotherapoes: Milestones, methods, and a new deployment-focused model. In E. D. Hibbs & S. P. Jensen (Eds.), *Psychosocial treatments for child and adolescent disorders: Empirically based strategies for clinical practice* (2nd ed., pp. 9–39). Washington, DC: American Psychological Association.

Westra, H. A., Dozois, D. J. A., & Marcus, M. (2007). Expectancy, homework compliance, and initial change in cognitive-behavioral therapy for anxiety. *Journal of Consulting and Clinical Psychology, 75*(3), 363–373.

White, K., & Davey, G. C. (1989). Sensory preconditioning and UCS inflation in human "fear" conditioning. *Behaviour Research and Therapy, 27*(2), 161–166.

Williams, J. M., Alatiq, Y., Crane, C., Barnhofer, T., Fennell, M. J., Duggan, D. S., et al. (2008). Mindfulness-based cognitive therapy (MBCT) in bipolar disorder: Preliminary evaluation of immediate effects on between-episode functioning. *Journal of Affective Disorders, 107,* 275–279.

Williams, S. L. (1990). Guided mastery treatment of agoraphobia: Beyond stimulus exposure. *Progress in Behavior Modification, 26,* 89–121.

Williams, S. L., & Zane, G. (1989). Guided mastery and stimulus exposure treatments for severe performance anxiety in agoraphobics. *Behaviour Research and Therapy, 27,* 237–245.

Wolpe, J. (1958). *Psychotherapy by reciprocal inhibition.* Oxford, England: Stanford University Press.

Young, J. E. (1990). *Cognitive therapy for personality disorders: A schema-focused approach.* Sarasota, FL: Professional Resource Press.

Young, J. E., Rygh, J. L., Weinberger, A. D., & Beck, A. T. (2008). Cognitive therapy for depression. In D. H. Barlow (Ed.), *Clinical handbook of psychological disorders: A step-by-step treatment manual.* New York: Guilford Press.

Zurawski, R. M., & Smith, T. W. (1987). Assessing irrational beliefs and emotional distress: Evidence and implications of limited discriminant validity. *Journal of Counseling Psychology, 34*(2), 224–227.

Index

About the Author

Michelle G. Craske received her PhD from the University of British Columbia in 1985. She has published extensively in the area of fear and anxiety disorders. She has written academic books on the topics of the etiology and treatment of anxiety disorders, gender differences in anxiety, and translation from the basic science of fear learning to the understanding and treating of phobias, in addition to several self-help books and therapist guides. She has been the recipient of continuous National Institute of Mental Health funding since 1993 for research projects pertaining to risk factors for anxiety disorders and depression among children and adolescents, the cognitive and physiological aspects of anxiety and panic attacks, neural mediators of behavioral treatments for anxiety disorders, fear extinction mechanisms of exposure therapy, and the development and dissemination of treatments for anxiety and related disorders. She was associate editor of the *Journal of Abnormal Psychology*, and she is presently associate editor of *Behaviour Research and Therapy* as well as a scientific board member for the Anxiety Disorders Association of America. She was a member of the DSM-IV Anxiety, Obsessive Compulsive Spectrum, Posttraumatic, and Dissociative Disorders Work Group, and chair of the Anxiety Disorders Subworkgroup. Dr. Craske has given invited keynote addresses at many international conferences and is frequently invited to present training workshops on the most recent advances in the cognitive–behavioral treatment for anxiety disorders. She is currently a professor in the Department of Psychology and Department of Psychiatry and Biobehavioral Sciences, UCLA, and director of the UCLA Anxiety Disorders Behavioral Research program.